THE PLAY OF HADRIAN THE SEVENTH

THE PLAY OF
HADRIAN VII

PETER LUKE

BASED ON

HADRIAN THE SEVENTH

AND OTHER WORKS BY

Fr. ROLFE (BARON CORVO)

* * *

ANDRE DEUTSCH

FIRST PUBLISHED 1968 BY
ANDRE DEUTSCH LIMITED
105 GREAT RUSSELL STREET
LONDON WCI
AND PENGUIN BOOKS LTD
HARMONDSWORTH, MIDDLESEX

PRINTED IN GREAT BRITAIN BY
COX AND WYMAN LIMITED
LONDON, READING AND FAKENHAM

SBN 233 96103 8

A Note on the Appearance and Behaviourisms
of Rolfe/Hadrian

Frederick William Rolfe, when the play opens, is a smallish, spare man, of about forty. He wears his greying hair very short, is myopic and can hardly see without his plain, steel-rimmed spectacles, but he is slim, agile and erect.

His tastes are austere but he is fond of such things as goat's milk, apples, raw carrots, fresh linen and particularly water, both to drink and to wash in. He is a practical man and carries a penknife with which he prepares his apples, sharpens pencils, etc.

He smokes a lot, always rolling his own and tucking the ends in with a pencil. Cat-like, his movements are swift, lithe and silent. Likewise, there are moments when he remains utterly still. As Pope, he comports himself with extraordinary dignity when the occasion demands, though 'off-duty' he reverts to his more abnormal self.

In the early part of Act I and at the end of the play, Rolfe wears a threadbare clerical grey suit. During the rest of the play, Rolfe/Hadrian wears such Canonical dress as may be appropriate.

Hadrian the Seventh received its first performance at the Birmingham Repertory Theatre on May 9, 1967. It had its first London performance at the Mermaid on April 18, 1968. Directed by Peter Dews and designed by Tim Goodchild, it had the following cast:

FREDERICK WILLIAM ROLFE	Alec McCowen
MRS NANCY CROWE	Margaret Courtenay
AGNES	Peggy Aitchison
1ST BAILIFF	Alan MacNaughtan
2ND BAILIFF	Donald Eccles
DR COURTLEIGH	Donald Eccles
DR TALACRYN	Alan MacNaughtan
JEREMIAH SANT	Patrick McAlinney
CARDINAL RAGNA	Brian Coburn
CARDINAL BERSTEIN	Otto Diamant
FATHER ST ALBANS	Brian Tully
RECTOR OF ST ANDREW'S COLLEGE	Aidan Turner
GEORGE ARTHUR ROSE	Vivian Mackerrell
CARDINAL ARCHDEACON	Paddy Ward
PAPAL CHAMBERLAIN	Patrick Marley

CARDINALS, PAPAL GUARDS, SWISS GUARDS, ACOLYTES, AND SEMINARISTS

Characters

FREDERICK WILLIAM ROLFE, *a spoilt priest. At opening of play, an impoverished writer in his forties. Later Pope Hadrian VII*

MRS NANCY CROWE, *his landlady. A shrewish, genteel widow. About forty*

AGNES, *a charwoman. A decent old body* *

1ST BAILIFF, *elderly, white-haired*★

2ND BAILIFF, *tall, amiable, in his forties*★

DR COURTLEIGH, CARDINAL-ARCHBISHOP OF PIMLICO, *elderly, white haired*★

DR TALACRYN, BISHOP OF CAERLEON, *tall, amiable, in his forties*★

JEREMIAH SANT, *an ultra-Protestant demagogue from Ulster. About fifty*

CARDINAL RAGNA, *Cardinal Secretary of State. A loud-mouthed, red-faced bull of a prelate. An Italian*

CARDINAL BERSTEIN, *a cold, arrogant German*

FATHER ST ALBANS, *an Englishman and Prepositor-General of the Jesuits. A sinister, sardonic man. He is known as the 'Black Pope' – an apt cognomen*

THE CARDINAL ARCHDEACON RECTOR OF ST ANDREW'S, *an opinionated old man who has spent a life-time of teaching and learnt nothing himself*

GEORGE ARTHUR ROSE, *a young seminarist at St Andrew's College, Rome. A good-looking, ascetic youth, as Rolfe might once have been*

EXTRAS, *Cardinals, Papal Guards, Chamberlains, Acolytes, etc.*

★At producer's discretion these four characters may be doubled, thus emphasizing Rolfe's subsequent fantasy.

ACT ONE

Scene One

FREDERICK ROLFE's *bed-sitting room in London. The set need do no more than suggest the abode of a poor scholar of fastidious habits and austere tastes.*

Required: A door, a plain table, a camp bed, a towel-horse, a shabby armchair, and a very small gas fire with a pay-as-you-burn meter. On the table, which is beside the chair, are a number of manuscripts, reference books, ink-pots, writing materials, etc. A screen decorated with outsize young male angels (Rolfe's work) faces the audience. Perhaps hanging somewhere should be a discreet crucifix. The door of the room is barricaded by a chair wedged under the door-handle.

As the curtain rises we see ROLFE *at his table addressing himself to his manuscript and smoking a fat, untidy home-rolled cigarette which he seldom takes out of his mouth. He shivers with the cold and gets up quickly to take a blanket off the bed which he drapes around his shoulders. He sits down again and continues to write.*

After a moment there is a knock on the door. ROLFE *looks round to make sure that the chair is firmly wedged in place and smirks with satisfaction. The knocking is repeated more peremptorily accompanied by rattlings at the door-handle.*

MRS CROWE [*off*]: Mr Rolfe. [*She tries the door-handle which doesn't give.*] Mr Rolfe. [*She rattles the door-handle.*] What's the matter with this door? . . . Mr Rolfe I know you're there.

ROLFE: Tickle your ass with a feather, Mrs Crowe.

MRS CROWE [*off*]: What did you say?

ROLFE: Particularly nasty weather, Mrs Crowe.

MRS CROWE: Mr Rolfe, I haven't climbed all these stairs just to be insulted. There are two gentlemen below who wish to see you.

ROLFE [*noticeably startled, jumps up*]: To see *me*?

MRS CROWE [*off*]: Yes, to see you.

[ROLFE *quickly takes the fag-end out of his mouth and crosses to the door to remove the barricade.* MRS CROWE *comes furiously in. She is a widow of about forty with pretentions to good looks and gentility. She succeeds only in being 'genteel'.* ROLFE *looks nervously past her down the staircase.*]

MRS CROWE: Ah, I thought you'd come off your high horse when you heard that.

ROLFE [*recovering slightly*]: Oh . . . well I'm very busy.

MRS CROWE: They said it was a private matter which couldn't wait.

ROLFE [*attempting to bluster*]: I'm not prepared to see them unless they state the precise nature of their business, Mrs Crowe.

MRS CROWE: If you think I'm going to run all the way up and down those stairs like a skivvy to carry your messages – [*Significantly*] – I think you'd better see them, Mr Rolfe.

ROLFE: Oh? Hmmm! Very well. Please show them up, Mrs Crowe, but let it be clearly understood –

[MRS CROWE *goes, shutting the door behind her.*]

– that I haven't got all day . . . Lascivious bitch!

[*As soon as* MRS CROWE *goes,* ROLFE *looks in the mirror and quickly puts on a stiff white collar and a plain black tie. He puts a packet of oatmeal out of sight and composes himself at the table to make notes from a lexicon.*]

I'm in an awful state. Come on, come on. Buck up. [*Hearing footsteps.*] Oh, my God . . .

[*Sounds of footsteps mounting the stairs and, with peremptory knock,* MRS CROWE *ushers in the callers who stand rather breathless in the door.* ROLFE *goes on making notes. After a moment he looks up.*]

[*Turning on the charm.*] Ah, good day, gentlemen. [*With a gracious nod to* MRS CROWE.] Thank you so much, Mrs Crowe.

[MRS CROWE *momentarily hovers in the hope of hearing something.*]

Please don't bother to wait. I shall see my visitors out myself.
[MRS CROWE *goes reluctantly.*

ROLFE draws himself up to the full extent of his inconsiderable height to receive his guests. A trembling knee only gives away his nervousness.]

And now, gentlemen, please tell me how I can be of service to you.

[*The* SECOND BAILIFF *is a venerable-looking old man with white hair. His colleague (*FIRST BAILIFF*) is a tall, amiable, healthy-looking fellow in his early forties. It is suggested that both should bear a resemblance to* DR COURTLEIGH, *Cardinal-Archbishop of Pimlico and* DR TALACRYN, *Bishop of Caerleon. Alternatively, the parts can be doubled to emphasize the likeness.*]

IST BAILIFF [*looking at document in his hand*]: Are you Mr Corvo?

ROLFE [*suspiciously*]: No.

IST BAILIFF [*looking at papers*]: Sorry, sir, I mean *Baron* Corvo?

ROLFE: That is not my name.

IST BAILIFF [*consulting papers*]: Oh. Then are you Frank W. Hochheimer?

ROLFE [*stiffly*]: No.

IST BAILIFF: Or Mr F. Austin?

ROLFE [*icily*]: I am not.

2ND BAILIFF: But you *are* Mr Frederick William *Rolfe*, [*He pronounces it as in 'golf'.*] are you not, sir?

ROLFE: That is almost correct, my name is Frederick William *Rolfe*. [*He pronounces it as in 'oaf'.*] And who, may I ask, are you?

IST BAILIFF: My colleague and I are Officers of the Courts – Bailiffs, you understand – and we hold a writ issued against you, Mr Rolfe, [*He hands* ROLFE *a document, who takes it and reads it.*] on behalf of various parties claiming certain debts. Do you follow me so far, Mr Rolfe?

ROLFE: Your brevity will assist my comprehension.

3

1ST BAILIFF: Quite so, sir. And I'm sure my colleague and I have no wish to remain here longer than necessary, so I will endeavour to constrict myself to the essential details, sir. The position is that, in brief, the Court has seen fit to award against you the initial sum of the debt plus the costs of the several plaintiffs versus Yourself for which a remittance must be made into Court forthwith in default of which and in consideration of A Warrant of Execution there will be no alternative but to attend at your premises and remove the contents thereof for sale by Public Auction.

ROLFE [*mumbles*]: And then throw dice for my garments.

1ST BAILIFF: I beg your pardon.

2ND BAILIFF [*who has been scrutinizing writ*]: 'Scuse me asking, but are you by any chance a clergyman or anything of that sort? I mean – Fr. Rolfe – it looks a bit like Father Rolfe. See what I mean?

ROLFE: My name is Frederick Rolfe. I have never taken Holy Orders. Had I done so, no doubt I should have been a Bishop by now – not a mere priest.

2ND BAILIFF [*guffawing good-naturedly*]: Ho, ho, sir. Very good.

1ST BAILIFF: Well, I think if you're quite clear as to the nature of our call, sir, we . . .

ROLFE: You leave me in no doubt as to the nature of your call.

1ST BAILIFF [*producing a slip of paper*]: In that case perhaps you'd be good enough to sign this undertaking not to remove your furniture or effects or any part thereof from the premises. Until further notice.

ROLFE: You're asking me to sign this document?

1ST BAILIFF: That's right, sir. Just here.

ROLFE: I'm sorry, but that's something I never do.

1ST BAILIFF: What's that, sir?

ROLFE: Sign documents. I never sign documents.

1ST BAILIFF: Purely a formality, sir, I assure you.

ROLFE: You can assure me till the Day of Judgement, as many others have done before. Invariably their assurances were

4

perfervid, perfidious, casuistic and, in a word, false. Ergo, no signature. Sorry.

1ST BAILIFF: Are you saying you are refusing to sign, sir?

ROLFE: I am saying in the simplest possible language that I do not intend to sign that document. Are you satisfied?

1ST BAILIFF: No, sir, I am not. And I should warn you that I don't think you are acting in your own best interest in taking this attitude.

ROLFE: If I had been acting in my own best interests in the past I should have withheld my signature on numerous other occasions. This would have saved me from being defrauded by various priests and publishers out of thousands of pounds.

1ST BAILIFF: I'm afraid I don't know about that, sir. But if you are refusing to sign this B 63 form here, I shall have no alternative but to apply immediately to the Court for a Warrant of Execution. You've not heard the last of this, I'm afraid, sir. Good day.

[*The* BAILIFFS *make for the door.*]

2ND BAILIFF: Good day, sir.

[*Etc. Ad lib*
Alone, ROLFE's *flippant demeanour suddenly changes to that of savage rage.*]

ROLFE [*through clenched teeth*]: Someone will have to suffer for this.

[MRS CROWE *appears at the door.*]

MRS CROWE: Are you by any chance speaking to me?

ROLFE [*quickly pulling himself together*]: If I had heard you knock, Mrs Crowe, I would have given myself the pleasure of addressing you, but since I did not –

MRS CROWE: Perhaps you would be good enough to tell me who your callers were, Mr Rolfe.

ROLFE: I'm not aware that it is part of our contract that I have to identify my visitors.

MRS CROWE: When your visitors are obviously policemen I consider that I have a right to know what is going on in my house. What am I supposed to think? What do you suppose other people are going to think?

ROLFE: Experience of the vilest kind has taught me to be pessimistic about the thinking capacity of my fellow men – and, need I add, women.

MRS CROWE: You're in trouble again, aren't you? Who were those men? Were they the police? They were, weren't they?

ROLFE: No.

MRS CROWE: Well, why wouldn't they give their names then? Is it money? [*Pause*] It is, isn't it?

ROLFE: How can it be anything else? Of course it's money.

MRS CROWE: So they were bailiffs then? [*There is a silence while* MRS CROWE *vacillates between her outraged feelings as a landlady and her concupiscent inclinations as a woman. Taking a step nearer to him. In a wheedling tone of voice.*] Why don't you let me help you? I could help you – if you wanted me to.

  [*She takes another step nearer and* ROLFE *backs away, only to find that his escape is blocked by the chair and table.*]

You know I have always wanted to be your friend. Couldn't I be now? Mr Crowe left me quite comfortable. You know that.

  [*She lays a hand on his arm but in his loathing of her touch he crashes back into the table and knocks it over. Books, papers and ink go all over the floor.* ROLFE *hurries to pick up the mess.*]

  [*Furious at the rejection of her advances*] There! Now look what you've done! Ink all over the floor! How do you suppose I'll ever get that out? It'll probably go right through to the ceiling below.

ROLFE [*picking things up*]: I will naturally make good any damage done.

MRS CROWE: Make good any damage! With the bailiffs hardly out of the house? [*Working herself up.*] I'm not fooled by your high-falutin talk any more. Before you do any more of your 'making good', you'll kindly pay me the quarter's rent you owe. Yes, and you'll kindly pay it by the end of the week as well or I shall be obliged to give you notice to leave. As a matter of fact, I need the room for a business gentleman.

ROLFE: A business *gentleman*? Is there such a thing?

MRS CROWE: Oh, perhaps *Baron Corvo* wouldn't call him a gentleman. But then Baron Corvo is an aristocrat . . . Or is he? I seem to remember a few shady deals that *that* fine gentleman tried to pull off . . . Oh yes, I've quite a good memory you know, Mr Rolfe – or should I say, Mr Austin . . . or Mr Hochheimer?

ROLFE: I would advise you to hold your tongue. You are talking of people who no longer exist.

MRS CROWE: Oh, don't they? Funnily enough, the gentleman I mentioned who is coming here knew them quite well, now that I come to think of it. Yes, he did.

ROLFE: I haven't the slightest idea what you're talking about, neither have I any desire to . . . Who is this person?

MRS CROWE: Oh I fancy you'll remember him all right. At least you should do, seeing that you once worked for him – that is till he had to get rid of you on account of your – er – behaviour . . . Don't you remember Belfast?

ROLFE: Sant!

MRS CROWE: That's right, Mr Rolfe. Mr Jeremiah Sant.

ROLFE: That Glengall Street gurrier!

MRS CROWE: I want the room.

ROLFE [*nervously; more to himself than to her*]: What does he want to come here for, tooting his Orange flute? What street corner is he going to bang his Lambeg drum on this time?

MRS CROWE: It's none of your business. I've said what I have to say. It's pay up or get out. [*She goes, deliberately not slamming the door.*]

ROLFE [*shouting in paroxysm of rage at the closed door*]: You can't get manure from a wooden rocking-horse, you rapacious, concupiscent – female. [*After a short pause he has second*

thoughts and runs to open the door – he shouts.] Mrs Crowe!
[*No answer.*]

Mrs Crowe, I know you're listening. When you're sorry
for what you've said, don't be afraid to say so ... Mrs
Crowe? ... Someone will have to suffer for this ... All
those curves and protuberances – breeding, that's all they're
good for ... Jeremiah Sant is a gerrymandering gouger! ...
[ROLFE *goes back into the room and puts the blanket round his
shoulders, shivering with rage, mortification and sheer cold. He
rolls and lights a cigarette and holds it cupped in his two hands
for the warmth.*

*After a moment he hears footsteps on the stairs again. He listens,
wondering if it is* MRS CROWE *coming back to apologize.
Instead a letter is thrust under the door. He looks at it suspiciously,
then picks it up and turns it over looking at the seal.*]

ROLFE: What ... What's that? ... Archbishop's House? [*He
tears the letter open, crosses himself, and reads it with trembling
hands.*]

ROLFE [*savagely*]: Hell and damnation! ... Imbeciles ...
Owl-like Hierarchs ... Degenerates ... [*Pause*] God, if ever
You loved me, hear me. They have denied me the priesthood
again. Not a chance do You give me, God – ever. Listen!
How can I serve You while You keep me so sequestered?
I'm intelligent. So, O God, You made me. But intelligence
must be active, potent and perforce I am impotent and in-
active always; futile in my loneliness. Why, O God, have
You made me strange, uncommon, such a mystery to my
fellow-creatures? Am I such a ruffian as to merit total exile
from them?

You have made me denuded of the power to love – to love
anybody or to be loved. I shall always be detached and apart
from the others. I suppose I must go on like that to the end –
[*Grimly*] because they are frightened of me – frightened of
the labels I put on them. [*He puts out his cigarette savagely.*]
Oh God, forgive me smoking. I quite forget. I am not doing

well at present. They force me into it: a pose of haughty genius, subtle, learned, inaccessible. Oh, it's wrong, wrong altogether, but what can I do? God, tell me, clearly unmistakably and distinctly, tell me, tell me what I must do – and make me do it . . . Oh Lord, I am sick – and very tired.

[*He lies down on the bed for a moment but his mind is in a ferment and he cannot rest. There is the sound of feet on the stairs again and then a knock at the door.*]

[*Fiercely, sitting up*] Who is it?

AGNES [*an elderly charlady*]: It's only me, sir.

ROLFE [*gently*]: Oh! All right. Come in, Agnes.

[*She comes in with tray. She wears working clothes and an overall.*]

AGNES: Oooh! You look a real dream of bliss, you do! I brought you a little bread-and-milk. Whatever have you been saying to the Missus? Oh, well never mind. Here you are. Eat it up whilst it's hot.

[*She puts down tray. On which is a bowl of bread-and-milk and a newspaper.*]

ROLFE: Thank you, Agnes. Please leave it on the table.

AGNES: My word, isn't it chilly in here? Why ever haven't you turned on the –

[*She takes a quick look at* ROLFE, *and seeing he's not paying attention, fumbles for her purse and from it takes a coin which she puts into the meter.* ROLFE *looks up and sees her.*]

ROLFE: Agnes, I forbid you –

AGNES [*taking matches from apron and lighting fire*]: Get along! Who d'you think you're forbidding then?

ROLFE [*coming over to warm himself*]: You're a dear good soul, Agnes, but you shouldn't have done that.

AGNES: Fiddlesticks! You can give it me back before I go to Mass Sunday –

ROLFE: But Agnes –

AGNES: I know you writing folk. I've had some in my time, don't think I haven't. All pride and no pence . . . not to mention the goings on . . .

ROLFE: I'm trying to tell you Agnes, that I may not be able to pay you back on Sunday. I'm destitute.

AGNES: Oh fiddle-de-dee. Sunday? I'm sure I never said *next* Sunday. Wait till the number comes up with your name on it and you can stand me a treat.

ROLFE: So I will, Agnes, my word on it. [*He crosses to the tray, picks up the bowl of bread-and-milk and starts to eat hungrily.*]

AGNES: I don't know why you don't go back to your painting. You had ever such a lovely touch with that . . .

[ROLFE *is still guzzling up the bread-and-milk when his eye falls on the newspaper. He picks it up and starts reading it, perfunctorily at first then with ever increasing interest.*]

AGNES: . . . all those saints large as life. Some of them larger, I wouldn't be surprised . . .

ROLFE: The Pope's dead.

AGNES [*not really listening*]: Then there was your photography. I'm sure you could make a bit out of that – but you haven't got your camera now, have you?

ROLFE: Agnes, the Pope is dead.

AGNES: What's that you say, dear?

ROLFE: Pope Leo XIII died yesterday, Agnes.

AGNES: Oooh, he never!

ROLFE [*reading from the paper*]: 'A Conclave of the Sacred College is to be convened immediately in order to elect a successor to the Holy See . . .'

AGNES: God rest his soul, the poor old gentleman. [*She crosses herself.*]

ROLFE [*continuing to read*]: 'In accordance with the Council of Lateran, the votes of two thirds of the Cardinals present at the Conclave will be required for the election of the Supreme Pontiff. A Vatican expert reports, however, that with the present alignment among the various factions in the Sacred College, it is by no means easy to see how a clear two-thirds majority can be achieved. He goes on to suggest . . .'

AGNES: Well I never. Perhaps they'll choose our own Archbishop this time. It's about time they had an English Pope for a change.

[ROLFE *turns to stare at her.*]

There ... I've finished you now, Mr Rolfe ... See you tomorrow then.

[ROLFE *stands staring after her for a brief moment. Then he crosses swiftly to the bookcase and takes out a fat-looking reference book and looks up something in the index. He appears to find what he wants for he then switches off the main light leaving on only the one by his work table. He crosses quickly to the table, takes up a ream of new foolscap paper and starts to write rapidly with occasional reference to the book.*]

ROLFE [*writing and thinking aloud*]: 771 to 795, Hadrian the First ... 867 to 872, Hadrian the Second ... 884 to 885 – not very long, that one – Hadrian the Third ... Ah, here we are! 1154 to 1159, Nicholas Breakspeare, Hadrian the Fourth, the first and only English Pope. Ha! Son of a monk. [*There's a pause while he flips through the reference book again.*] Hadrian the Fifth, a Genoese. Hadrian the Sixth, that's right, from Utrecht. [*He continues to write with great energy for a moment or two.*] Hadrian the Fourth ... Hadrian the Fifth ... Hadrian the Sixth ... In mind he was tired, worn out, by years of hope deferred, of loneliness, of unrewarded toil. In body he was almost prostrate. .... [*He goes on working with great concentration. Then, once more, he is interrupted by a knock at the door.*] Who is it?

MRS CROWE [*off, sounding ingratiating*]: It's only me, Mr Rolfe.

ROLFE: Oh. What do you want, Mrs Crowe?

MRS CROWE: Please may I come in, Mr Rolfe. There's two gentlemen to see you.

ROLFE: What? Come in.

MRS CROWE [*entering*]: There are two gentlemen downstairs to see you. They're clergymen.

ROLFE: Clergymen. What sort of clergymen?

MRS CROWE: I couldn't really say. One's an elderly gentleman all in red and black. The other is much younger with bits of purple.

ROLFE: His Grace the Archbishop of Pimlico, and the Bishop of Caerleon . . . of course.

MRS CROWE [*more intrigued than ever*]: Oh, really. You were expecting them then?

ROLFE: They are not entirely unexpected. Now perhaps you would be good enough to . . .

MRS CROWE: I hope you don't mind my asking, but are they friends of yours?

ROLFE: Mrs Crowe –

MRS CROWE: Yes, I'll bring them up.

> [*As soon as* MRS CROWE *has gone*, ROLFE *rushes to put on a stiff collar and black tie. This done, he quickly adopts a dignified posture to receive his visitors.*
>
> *After a pause* MRS CROWE *shows in* DR COURTLEIGH *and* DR TALACRYN.]

MRS CROWE: This way gentlemen. I'm sorry for all the stairs. Oh dear, I'm quite out of breath myself.

ROLFE: *Thank* you, Mrs Crowe.

MRS CROWE: I just wondered if your guests would like something . . .

ROLFE: Not for the moment, thank you.

MRS CROWE: Very well. I'll leave the tea things out so that you can help yourselves later. [*Goes out.*]

> [ROLFE *waits for the door to shut behind* MRS CROWE. *He then goes straight to* TALACRYN, *kneels to him and kisses the Episcopal ring on his hand.*]

TALA: Your Eminence, may I present Mr Rolfe.

ROLFE [*rising. To* COURTLEIGH]: Your Eminency will understand that I do not wish to be disrespectful, but the Bishop of Caerleon calls himself my friend.

COURT: I hope, Mr Rolfe, that you will accept my blessing as well as Dr Talacryn's.

> [ROLFE *kneels and kisses the Cardinalatial ring.*]

ROLFE: Please sit down – as best you may.

[*Their* EMINENCES *sort themselves out under the slightly proscribed circumstances.*]

TALA: Freddy, His Eminence wishes to ask you a few questions and he thought you would not take it amiss if I were present – as your friend.

[ROLFE *acknowledges* TALACRYN's *remark and turns to the* CARDINAL.]

ROLFE: I have been imagining Your Eminency in Rome – at the Conclave.

COURT: I was there until very recently; and then – well, you are said to be an expert in the annals of conclaves, Mr Rolfe, so it will interest you to know that we stand adjourned.

ROLFE: Adjourned, Eminency?

COURT: Yes Mr Rolfe adjourned. But how do you – how could anybody possibly know? There has been nothing of it in the newspapers.

ROLFE: You were good enough to say Eminency that I have made some little study of the annals of conclaves. I have also studied the form of those members of the Sacred College who could be said to be possible starters for the Supreme Pontificate.

TALA [*to* COURT]: A sporting metaphor, your Eminence, indicating –

COURT: I am sufficiently acquainted with the jargon of the Turf to understand what Mr Rolfe is saying. Do go on Mr Rolfe.

ROLFE: Then, if I may continue the analogy, it is perfectly plain to a student of these matters that the short-odds favourite for the Throne of St Peter must be the present Secretary of State of the Vatican, Cardinal Ragna, whom God preserve.

COURT: Not everyone would say 'amen' to that I fear,

ROLFE: – but, there is a malpractice called 'Bumping and Boring', much frowned upon by the stewards, and I very much doubt if your Eminencies in the Sacred College

13

would allow Cardinal Ragna to trot away with the race.

COURT: Eh?

ROLFE: – and I'm prepared to bet a thousand pounds to a penny-halfpenny stamp that the reason your Eminency is back here in London is because the Conclave has broken down having failed to achieve a clear two-thirds majority for that very reason.

COURT: Bless my soul, the man's right, Frank. [TALACRYN *looks pleased at the impression made by his protégé.*] Ragna was – ah – 'nobbled', I believe the phrase is.

ROLFE: – and furthermore I'm prepared to wager something even more valuable, namely my shirt, that the Sacred College, having failed to elect a Pope in the normal manner, has now decided to proceed by the Way of Compromise, thus scotching Ragna. Would I be right, Eminency?

COURT: You would, you would. [*To* TALA.] The man's a genius, Frank.

ROLFE: – and just to bring off the Treble Event I would put my accumulated winnings on the fact that your Eminence has been chosen as one of the nine Cardinals Compromissory who now have between you the awful task of choosing a Pope from any man upon this earth.

COURT [*now really worried*]: I beg you, Mr Rolfe – no, no, as your Archbishop I command you – to say nothing of this surmise to a soul. Can I depend upon you, Mr Rolfe?

TALA: I feel sure you can count on Mr Rolfe's absolute discretion, Your Eminence.

ROLFE: I don't think you can count on it at all. Let me get you some tea. [*He abruptly leaves the room.*]

COURT [*sotto voce*]: Remind me quickly, Frank, why your friend Rolfe was debarred from Holy Orders.

TALA: The uncompromising testimony of his Diocesan, Eminence, that he has no Vocation.

COURT: Yes, yes, yes. We know the formula. But more specifically . . .

TALA: Well that is always a little difficult. Without immediate access to the documents . . .

COURT: Come to the point, man. I must know in order to proceed.

TALA: Yes, well, if my memory serves me, there was some question of credit obtained, debts not honoured – that sort of thing.

COURT: Frailties and deplorable, but hardly sufficient to earn an unequivocal 'No Vocation'. What else?

TALA: Else? There is nothing else that I give credence to.

COURT: But there are suspicions, rumours of impurity perhaps . . .

TALA: I have no suspicions and I listen to no rumours. I know only the man, Eminence. In spite of the discouragement he has received from all sides he has persisted for twenty years with the belief in his Divine Vocation.

COURT: That would presuppose obstinacy rather than intelligence.

TALA: Obstinate he may be, but one can hardly deny his intelligence. I would remind you that he is an expert on St Augustine, he has The Enchiridion at his fingertips and his knowledge of Dogmatic and Moral Theology surpasses that of a number of Bishops.

COURT: You could say the same about the Devil.

TALA [*permits himself a laugh*]: Your Eminence is not easy to convince. I grant that there is, as it were, a satanic quality about Rolfe, but there are two Rolfes: one a sort of demon with a prediliction for Sainthood; the other a Saint with a strong proclivity towards the Devil.

COURT: And which would you have me reinstate as a Clerk in Holy Orders?

TALA: It is my belief that if he were given the chance to pursue what he has so long maintained to be his Vocation, it is the Saint that would finally emerge.

COURT: Hmmmm! And must I spin a coin with Old Nick to

decide the matter? No, Frank, I do not think so. Genius or madman, Saint or Messenger from Beelzebub, I have examined your case and I have examined my own conscience, but I cannot find –

TALA: Did your Eminence ever reflect – with respect – that very few clergymen are capable of forming an unprejudiced judgement on the evidence before them and on nothing else?

COURT: It is true that on re-examining the matter I became convinced that a wrong had been done.

TALA: An immense and irreparable wrong, Eminence.

COURT: You put your case very strongly, Frank.

TALA: I cannot put it strongly enough, Eminence. By denying this man to the service of God, we may also be denying God to the man.

COURT: I think I am about to regret ever having heard the name of Frederick William Rolfe.

TALA [*in a low voice*]: I think I hear him coming.

[ROLFE *enters with a tea tray.*]

ROLFE: There's nothing like China tea and hot buttered toast –

COURT: I am extremely fond of hot buttered toast.

ROLFE: – unfortunately, the Commissariat here only runs to the tea.

COURT: Oh! Ah! – doubtless the ravens will provide eh!

ROLFE: My experience has been to the contrary.

COURT: Oh!

[*Business of handing round tea. Ad lib remarks about 'One lump or two', etc.*]

COURT [*sipping tea*]: Ah! – these are – very pregnant times, Mr Rolfe.

ROLFE: Times always are, Eminency.

[TALACRYN *signals a warning to* ROLFE, '*not to be facetious*'.]

COURT: Quite. Well perhaps you will now permit me to come to the point I wished to – ah – consult you upon.

[ROLFE *bows acknowledgement.*]

COURT: It has recently been brought to my remembrance that

16

you were at one time a candidate for Holy Orders, Mr Rolfe.
I am aware of all the – ah – unpleasantness which attended
that portion of your career; but it is only lately that I have
fully realized that you yourself have never accepted or
acquiesced in, the verdict of your superiors.

ROLFE: I never have accepted it. I have never acquiesced in it.
I never will accept it. I never will acquiesce in it.

COURT: Quite, er . . .

ROLFE: But – I nourish no grudge and seek no revenge. No,
nor even Justice. I am content to lead my own life, avoiding
all my brother Catholics when circumstances throw them
    [COURTLEIGH gets restive]
in my path. I don't squash cockroaches.

COURT: And the effect upon your own soul . . .?

ROLFE: The effect on my soul is perfectly ghastly. I have lost
faith in man, and I have lost the power of loving. I have become a rudderless derelict.

COURT: How terrible!

ROLFE: Terrible? Yes it is indeed terrible. And, as head of the
Roman Communion in this country, let the blame be upon
you for the destruction of this soul.
    [COURTLEIGH raises his hands in protest.]
As for your myrmidons, I spit upon them and defy them and
you may rest assured that I shall continue to fight them as
long as I can hold a pen.

COURT: Would you mind telling me your reasons?

ROLFE: I should have to say very disagreeable things, Eminence.

COURT: Tell me the truth.

ROLFE: The Catholic and Apostolic Church, with its cham-
pioning of learning and beauty, was always to be a real and
living thing. It was with the highest hopes, therefore, that I
entered Oscott College to begin my career as a Clerk in Holy
Orders. I was soon obliged to leave, however, after a dispute
with the Principal who seemed to see no offence in grubs
grazing on the lettuces and caterpillars cantering across the

17

refectory table. The Archbishop of Agneda then invited me, on recommendation, to attend St Andrew's College at Rome. I gladly went, on the assurance that my expenses would be borne by the Archbishop. They never were and, in consequence, I was several hundred pounds out of pocket.

COURT: Dear me! [*He looks at* TALACRYN *for confirmation, who nods agreement.*] Yes?

ROLFE: Then after four months in College, I was expelled suddenly and brutally.

COURT: And what reason was given?

ROLFE: No reason was ever given. The gossip of my fellow students – immature cubs given to acne and dog latin – was that I had no Vocation.

COURT: I see. Go on.

ROLFE: Then there was the occasion in Wales when the machinations of a certain cleric, whose cloven hoof defiled the shrine of the Blessed Saint Winefred of Holywell, defrauded me of my rightful deserts for two years of arduous work undertaken at his request. Having been robbed by the said priest not only of my means of livelihood, but also of health, comfort, friends and reputation, and brought physically to my knees, he then gave me the *coup de grace* by debarring me from the Sacraments. I then had no option but to leave Wales and start life from scratch. I walked to London. Two hundred and fourteen miles. It took me eighteen days.

COURT: Good gracious! But did no one come forward to assist you at this time?

ROLFE: No one except the Bishop of Caerleon who somewhat belatedly received me back into Communion.

[COURTLEIGH *looks at* TALACRYN *Bishop of Caerleon who avoids his glance.*]

Eventually, others, moved no doubt by the last twitchings of their dying consciences made tentative overtures. To these I quoted St Matthew XXV, 41–43.

COURT: Now, how does that go? [*He gropes in the air for the quotation.*]

ROLFE: From: 'I was hungered and ye gave me no meat' down to 'Depart from me ye cursed, into aeonial fire'.

COURT: You are hard, Mr Rolfe, very hard.

ROLFE: I am what you and your fellow Catholics have made me.

COURT: Poor child – poor child.

ROLFE: I request that Your Eminence will not speak to me in that tone. I disdain your pity at this date. The catastrophe is complete.

COURT: My son, have you never caught yourself thinking kindly of your former friends? You cannot always be in a state of white hot rage, you know.

ROLFE: Yes, Eminence, there are some with whom, strange to say, I would wish to be reconciled – when my anger is not dynamic, that is. [*He smiles.*] But they do not come to me – as you have come.

COURT: They probably do not wish to expose themselves to – ah – quotations from St Matthew's gospel.

ROLFE: Did I heave china-ware at your Lordship?

TALA: You did not. Your Eminence, I believe I understand Mr Rolfe's frame of mind. A burned child dreads the fire.

COURT: True. A cliché, but true. [*To* ROLFE] And what course did you embark on then, Mr Rolfe?

ROLFE: I determined to occupy my energies with some pursuit for which my nature fitted me, until the Divine Giver of my Vocation should deign to manifest it to others as well as myself. I took to painting and writing.

COURT [*patronizingly*]: And how did you sustain life in those precarious professions, pray?

TALA: To my knowledge, Your Eminence, Mr Rolfe began life again with no more than the clothes on his back, a book of the Hours and eight pounds in his pocket.

COURT: I'm obliged to you, but I wish to hear the details from Mr Rolfe himself.

ROLFE: I don't know how I kept alive the first winter. I only remember that I endured it in light summer clothes, since I had no others.

COURT: It was a hard winter.

ROLFE: But I didn't die, and I began to write simply because, by this time, I had an imperious necessity to say certain things. In any case, ultimate penury denied me access to painting materials. So literature is now the only outlet you Catholics have left me – and believe me, I have very much to say.

COURT: You have perhaps not many kindly feelings towards me personally, Mr Rolfe?

ROLFE: I trust that I shall never be found wanting in reverence to your Sacred Purple. But I am only speaking to you civilly now because you are a successor of Augustine and Theodore and Dunstan and Anselm, and because for the nonce, my friend the Bishop of Caerleon has made you my guest.

COURT: Well, well!

ROLFE: My Lord Cardinal, I do not know what you want of me, nor why you have come.

COURT: I wished first of all to know if you still remained Catholic.

ROLFE: If I still remained Catholic!

COURT: People who have been denied the priesthood have been known to commit apostasy.

ROLFE: Rest assured, Eminence, I am not in revolt against the Faith, but against the Faithful.

COURT [*trying not to get angry*]: I am trying to determine whether or not, at the time of which we are speaking, you formed any opinion of your own concerning your Vocation, Mr Rolfe.

ROLFE: No.

COURT: No?

ROLFE: No. My opinion concerning my Vocation for the priesthood had been formed when I was a boy of fifteen. I have never relinquished my Divine Gift.

COURT: You persist?

ROLFE: Your Eminence, I am not a bog-trotting Fenian or one of your Sauchiehall Street hybrids – but English and sure; born under Cancer. Naturally I persist.

COURT: But the man to whom Divine Providence vouchsafes a Vocation is bound to pursue it. *You* are practising as an author.

ROLFE: This is only a means to an end. When I shall have earned enough to pay my debts I shall go straight to Rome and fix the profligate prelate who sacked me.

COURT [*throwing up his hands*]: Sh-h!

TALA [*quickly*]: Your Eminence mustn't be offended by Mr Rolfe's satirical turn of phrase.

ROLFE: I beg Your Eminence's pardon for having spoken inurbanely, and [*to* TALA.] I thank Your Lordship for interpreting me so generously. But I have been abused for so long that I'm as touchy as a hornet with a brand-new sting.

TALA: Mr Rolfe, Your Eminence, is not the man to smite those who have done him ill.

ROLFE: Do not deceive yourself, My Lord. So long as we recruit our spiritual pastors from the hooligan class, I shall smite them with all my strength.

COURT: Really, Mr Rolfe!

TALA: You're a little beside the point, Freddy.

ROLFE: Under the circumstances, His Eminence will indulge me. I've had enough of being buffeted by bishops. Until I'm the possessor of a cheque book I do not propose to start commerce with the clergy again.

[*There is a pause while the* CARDINAL *looks into space and the* BISHOP *looks at his toes. Then:*]

COURT: Frederick William Rolfe, I summon you to offer yourself to me.

[*Pause*]

ROLFE [*quietly*]: I am not ready to offer myself to Your Eminence.

COURT: Not ready?

ROLFE: I hope I had made it clear that, in regard to my Vocation, I am marking time until I shall have earned enough to pay my debts which were so monstrously incurred on me.

COURT: You keep harping on that string.

ROLFE: It is the only string you have left unbroken on my lute.

COURT: Well, well: the money question need not trouble you.

ROLFE: But it does trouble me. And your amazing summons troubles me as well. Why do you come to me after all these years?

COURT: It is precisely because of these years – how many was it?

ROLFE: Call it twenty.

COURT: – that we must take your singular persistency as proof of the genuineness of your Vocation. And, therefore, I am here today to summon you to accept Holy Orders with no delay beyond the canonical intervals.

ROLFE: In two years' time, when I shall have published three more books, I will respond to your summons. Not till then.

TALA: But His Eminence has said that the money question need not hinder you.

ROLFE: Yes and the Archbishop of Agneda said the same.

[DR COURTLEIGH *looks as if he is going to explode and* DR TALACRYN *hastens to intervene.*]

TALA: I am witness of His Eminence's words, Freddy.

ROLFE: What's the good of that? Supposing in a couple of months His Eminence chooses to alter his mind? Could I hail a prince of the church before a secular tribunal? Would I? Could I subpoena Your Lordship to testify against your

Metropolitan and Provincial? Could I? Would I? Would You?

[COURTLEIGH *makes as if to interject but* ROLFE *cuts in.*]
My Lord Cardinal, I must speak, and you must hear me. You are offering me the Priesthood on good and legitimate grounds, for which I thank God. But if I correctly interpret you, you are also offering me something in the shape of money and I will be no man's pensioner.

COURT [*very mildly*]: Please understand me, Mr Rolfe, that the monies in question are being offered solely as restitution for the years in which you were denied the Priesthood.

ROLFE: On! [*Pause.*] No, I will not take charity.

TALA: Well, then, Freddy, in what form will you accept this act of justice from us. Do make an effort to believe we are sincerely in earnest and that in this matter we are in your hands. [*Turning to* COURTLEIGH] I may say that Your Eminence?

COURT: Unreservedly.

[*There is a pause while* ROLFE *considers.*]

ROLFE [*quietly but with determination*]: I will accept a written expression of regret for the wrongs which have been done to me by both Your Eminence and by others who have followed your advice, command or example.

COURT [*takes a folded piece of paper from his breviary*]: It is here.

ROLFE [*at first surprised, then reads with care*]: I thank Your Eminence. [*He lights it on the gas-fire and lets it burn.*]

COURT: Man alive!

ROLFE: I do not care to preserve a record of my superiors' humiliation.

COURT [*with an effort*]: I see that Mr Rolfe knows how to behave nobly, Frank.

ROLFE: Only now and again. But I had long ago arranged to do just that.

[*The* PRELATES *make a gesture of incomprehension to each other. They stand up to go.* ROLFE *kneels qnd receives benedictions.*]

T – B   23

COURT: We shall see you then at Archbishop's House to-morrow morning, Mr Rolfe.

ROLFE: I will be there at half-past seven to confess to the Bishop of Caerleon. Your Eminence says Mass at eight and will give me Holy Communion. Then, if it pleases Your Eminence, you will give me the four Minor Orders. In the meantime, I will go and have a Turkish bath and buy myself a Roman collar.

[*The* PRELATES *start to leave, led by* COURTLEIGH. ROLFE *opens the door and* COURTLEIGH *goes through.* TALACRYN *is about to follow when he is addressed by* ROLFE.]

Your Lordship doesn't happen to know the price of collars these days?

TALA [*apologetic*]: I haven't the slightest idea, I'm afraid.

ROLFE: Well then, just to be on the safe side, perhaps you wouldn't mind springing me a fiver.

TALA: Oh, certainly. Certainly.

[*Embarrassed,* TALACRYN *fumbles in his pockets for his wallet. Eventually he finds it and gives a banknote to* ROLFE *who accepts it graciously.*]

TALA: Thank you.

ROLFE: Not at all. See you tomorrow.

[TALACRYN *goes and* ROLFE *rolls himself a cigarette from the dottels on the ashtray. Having lit it, he claps his hands and proceeds energetically to do his exercises. (Knees bend, arms raising forwards, sideways and upwards with cigarette in mouth.)*]

ROLFE [*getting up from last 'knees bend'*]: What a blooming lark!

[*He crosses to mirror, takes off his tie and turns his collar back to front. He then gives his reflection an episcopal blessing. Suddenly he freezes. He sees a reflection of somebody behind him. He turns round to see* JEREMIAH SANT *standing in the doorway.*]

Sant!

SANT: Still at your play-acting, I see! What part is it this time?

ROLFE: What are you doing in here?

SANT: I've come to look at my room.

ROLFE: *Your* room?

SANT: Aye. I've been given to understand that you've got your marching orders again.

ROLFE: What do you mean?

SANT: The Order of the Boot. You're out. Just like old times, isn't it?

ROLFE [*changing tactics*]: Yes, as a matter of fact I do have to leave here as it happens. I've been summoned for work elsewhere.

SANT: Summoned, have ye? Summonsed, more likely, from what I know of you.

ROLFE: Meanwhile this room is mine until the end of the week.

SANT: Aye, if you've paid the rent.

ROLFE: Get out of here.

SANT: Oh, aye. I'm going, but I'll be back on Saturday so make sure you're away by then.

ROLFE: Why do you persist in hounding me?

SANT: I'll tell you a wee story. You'll mind Belfast down by the docks where the shipyard workers live?

ROLFE: It is not a memory I particularly cherish.

SANT: Aye, likely not. [*Pause for the painful memory to sink in.*] Well, we lived in one of those streets when I was a young feller. The houses were all painted the same colours – green and brown in good oil paint – because those were the colours of the ship they were building in the yard at the time.

ROLFE: I'm not interested in the social anthropology of Belfast.

SANT: Maybe: but I'll tell ye all the same. Ours was a Protestant street, you see, and on a blank wall at the end of it was a life-size portrait of King Billy – William of Orange to you – riding into battle on a white charger against the Popeheads.

ROLFE: That was Cargill Street and one of your wittier co-religionists had also painted 'Kick the Pope' on a gable-end.

SANT: I'm coming to who kicks who in a minute. The next street to ours was a Catholic street . . .

ROLFE: Paintwork by courtesy of the Cunard Steam-ship Company.

SANT: Let me finish. One day my wee brother Sam – he was only eleven years old at the time – wandered down that street. God knows why, but he did. He got into a fight. Some elder boys joined in. Those Papishes got him down on the ground and they kicked him. They went on kicking him till he stopped moving.

ROLFE: I heard.

SANT: Aye, they left him for dead. But he wasn't – not quite. Whenever I'm back in Belfast I go and see him at the asylum. He was thirty-two last birthday but he's still only eleven in his mind. Just lately he's taken to wetting his bed again.

ROLFE: Tragic. But one act of hooliganism begets another.

SANT: That may be what you call it. But, an eye for an eye and a tooth for tooth, saith the Lord . . . and I'm still biding my time. [*He makes for the door.*] When you go leave the window wide will ye. It's the smell of a Papish I can't abide. [*He goes out leaving the door open, singing 'The Sash my Father Wore'.*]

> 'Our Fathers knew the Rome of old
> And evil is thy fame,
> Thy kind embrace the galling chain,
> Thy kiss the blazing flame.'

ROLFE *stands quite still for a moment. His triumphant mood has vanished and, once more, he looks trapped and hunted. After a moment's thought he springs into action. Pulling a hold-all from under the bed, he throws his few effects into it quickly. He crosses to the door and listens to make sure the coast is clear. Having satisfied himself on this count, he picks up the hold-all and tip-toes out.*

Scene Two

A room in Archbishop House at 7.30 the following morning. A clock strikes the half-hour. TALACRYN *and* ROLFE *enter.*

TALA: Good morning, Freddy. I hope your new lodgings are comfortable.

ROLFE: Compared to Broadhurst Gardens they are as the Elysian Fields.

TALA: I never cared much for N.W.6 either. Now . . . shall we get this over?

ROLFE: It may take rather a long time.

TALA: All day if necessary.

> [TALACRYN *takes a small violet stole which he has been carrying on his arm, kisses the cross embroidered on it, and puts it round his shoulders. He takes a chair and sits.* ROLFE *kneels so that he is facing a three-quarter back view of the Bishop. He makes the sign of the cross (both skip through the ritual beginning and end of confession pretty fast).*]

ROLFE: Bless me, O Father, for I have sinned.

TALA: May the Lord be in thine heart and on thy lips, that thou with truth and humility mayest confess thy sins, [*Sign of the cross.*] in the name of the Father and of the Son, and of the Holy Ghost. Amen.

ROLFE: I last confessed five days ago.

TALA: Since then, my son?

ROLFE: Since then I broke the first commandment by being superstitiously silly enough to come downstairs in my socks because I had accidentally put on my left shoe before my right. I broke the third commandment by permitting my mind to be distracted by the palpably Dublin accent of the Priest who said Mass on Saturday.

TALA: Is there any more on your conscience, my son?

ROLFE: Lots. I confess that I have broken the sixth com-

27

mandment by continuing to read an epigram in the Anthology after I had found out that it was obscene. I have broken the third commandment of the Church by eating dripping toast for tea on Friday. I was hungry; it was very nice: I made a good meal of it and couldn't eat any dinner. This was thoughtless at first, then wilful.

TALA: Are you bound to fast this Lent?

ROLFE: Yes, Father . . . I should now like to make a general confession of the chief sins of my life.

TALA: Proceed my son.

ROLFE: I earnestly desire to do God's will in all things but I often fail. I like to worship my Maker alone, unseen of all save Him. That is why I cannot hear Mass with devotion in those churches where one is obliged to squat in a pew like a Protestant, with other people's hot and filthy breath blowing down my neck. My mind has a twist towards frivolity, towards perversity. I have been irreverent and disobedient to my superiors. For example, I said that the legs of a certain domestic prelate were formed like little Jacobean communion-rails.

[TALACRYN *reacts slightly to this last.*]

I have told improper stories – not of the revolting kind, but those which are witty, anti-protestant or recondite – the sort common among the clergy. Being antipathetic to fish, I once made an enemy sick by the filthy comparison which I used in regard to some oysters which he was about to eat. I confess that two or three times in my life I have delighted in impure thoughts inspired by some lines in Cicero's Oration for Marcus Coelius.

TALA: I don't for the moment recall – well never mind. Is there anything further?

ROLFE: There is one thing which I have never mentioned in confession except in vague terms only.

TALA: Relieve your mind, my son.

ROLFE: Father, I confess I have not kept my senses in proper custody. Sometimes I catch myself extracting elements of aesthetic enjoyment from unaesthetic situations.

TALA: Can you be more precise, my son?

ROLFE: Yes. Well, for example I once was present at the amputation of a leg. Under anaesthetics, directly the saw touched the marrow of the thigh bone, the other leg began to kick. I was next to it, and the surgeon told me to hold it still. It was ghastly but I did. And then I actually caught myself admiring the exquisite silky texture of the human skin ... Father, I am a very sorry Christian. I confess all these sins, all the sins which I cannot remember, all the sins of my life. I implore pardon of God; and from thee, O Father, penance and absolution. [*Quickly.*] Therefore, I beseech blessed Mary Ever-Virgin, Blessed Michael Archangel, Blessed John Baptist, the Holy Apostles, Peter and Paul, all saints and thee, O Father, to pray for me to the Lord our God.

TALA: My son, do you love God?

[*From silence, tardily the response emerges.*]

ROLFE: I don't know. I really don't know ... He is Maker of the World to me. He is Truth and Righteousness and Beauty. He is first. He is last. He is Lord of all to me. I absolutely believe in Him. I unconditionally trust Him. I am ready and willing to make any kind of sacrifice for Him. So far I clearly see. Then in my mind, there comes a great gap – filled with fog.

TALA: Do you love your neighbour?

ROLFE: What? ... Who?

TALA: Do you love your neighbour?

ROLFE: No. Frankly I detest him – and her. Most people are repulsive to me, because they are ugly in person, or in manner, or in mind. I have met those with whom I should like to be in sympathy, but I have been unable to get near enough to them.

TALA: Could you not love them?

ROLFE: No.

TALA: Do you love yourself?

ROLFE: On the whole, I think I despise myself, body, mind and soul. I do look after my body and cultivate my mind. And naturally I stick up for myself but – no, my body and mind are no particular pleasure to me.

TALA: Have you anything else to confess, my son?

ROLFE: Nothing. Really nothing. Father, I'm very tired. I long to be at rest.

TALA: That is actually the longing of your soul for God. Cultivate that longing, my son, for it will lead you to love Him. Thank Him with all your heart for this great gift of longing. At the same time remember the words of Christ our Saviour: 'If ye Love Me, keep My Commandments'. Remember, He definitely commands you to love your neighbour. Serve the servants of God, and you will learn to love God.

You have tasted the pleasures of this world and they are as ashes in your mouth. In the tremendous dignity to which you have been called – the dignity of the priesthood, you will be subject to fiercer temptations than those which have assaulted you in the past. Brace the great natural strength of your will to resist them. Begin to love your neighbour so that you may soon consciously come to love God. My son, the key to all your difficulties, past, present, and to come, is love . . . for your penance you will say – no the penance for minor orders is rather long – for your penance you will say the Divine Praises with the celebrant after Mass . . . and now say after me: [*This ritual is gabbled through.*] O my God, most worthy of all love –

ROLFE: O my God, most worthy of all love – I grieve from my heart for having sinned against Thee – And I purpose by Thy Grace . . . Never more to offend Thee for the time to come.

TALA: *Ego te absolvo* [*Sign of the Cross.*] *in Nomine Patris et Filii et Spiritus Sancti.* Amen. Go in peace and pray for me.

[ROLFE *and* TALACRYN *rise.* TALACRYN *resumes his informal manner.*]

... but before you do, I have been instructed by His Eminence to inform you that you will accompany him to Rome tomorrow. You will act as his private chaplain at the Conclave. We will travel together, Freddy.

[*A single bell starts to toll insistently. An echoing Litany is distantly heard.*]

LIGHTS FADE

Scene Three

Light up.

A Chapel in Vatican.

A bell tolls in distance. A Liturgy is being intoned in some remote side chapel.

Two ACOLYTES *(boys) in surplices enter from opposite wings, genuflect in unison towards direction of altar, and proceed to light candelabra with long tapers. Having done so they go out together after another genuflection.*

TALACRYN *and* ROLFE *now enter together. Hands folded clasping breviaries.* ROLFE, *now in Holy Orders, wears black soutane and biretta.* TALACRYN *wears similar garb suitable to a bishop. (Soutane and red cap, cape and cummerbund?) They perambulate.*

ROLFE [*sniffing at smell of incense*]: Nothing stinks like the odour of sanctity.

TALA: Now, now.

ROLFE: Look at those frescoes. Wasn't it Mark Twain who said: 'The Creator made Italy from designs by Michael-angelo'?

TALA [*distrait*]: Very possibly ... Their Eminences are still sitting, it seems...

ROLFE: On two addled eggs apiece.

TALA: Freddy, I beg you ... the whole world is waiting for the imminent announcement of a new Pope, and you make jokes in rather doubtful taste.

ROLFE: Let me assure Your Lordship that my flippancy in no way reflects my concern with the outcome of the Sacred Consistory.

TALA: If the reactionaries have their way and Ragna is elected it is my belief that it would set the Church back a hundred years.

ROLFE: My own anxiety on this score is somewhat mitigated by the determination of our own Archbishop to thwart this move at any cost. Courtleigh would nominate the Parish Priest of Ballyjamesduff if it would keep Ragna out.

TALA [*smiling*]: I wish I had it in me to be quite so irreverent as you, Freddy.

ROLFE: Perhaps, but I doubt if Your Lordship has it in him to be quite so devout either. You are a natural Christian, my Lord Bishop. I, on the other hand, am a religious maniac.

TALA: You do yourself an injustice.

ROLFE [*casually*]: I know I do. [*Looking up at fresco on ceiling.*] Isn't that superb! [*Pointing.*] Look at that. A little lacking in generosity in describing ... [*He makes a graphic gesture*] ... but compared to a figure like that, what can people see to admire in the female form?

TALA: It's a matter of taste, I suppose.

ROLFE [*looking at* TALACRYN]: What a waste!

TALA: What is a waste?

ROLFE: That such a fine upstanding man as Your Lordship should have felt inclined to accept the celibacy of priesthood.

TALA: Good Heavens, Freddy. If you are being serious, I can assure you that from the moment I took Orders no other thought ever occurred to me.

ROLFE: Nevertheless one has to admit that the vestigal nipples on a man are about as useful as the Pontifical pudenda. Had I been a Renaissance Pope, I would have insisted that –

[*A bell begins to clang insistently.*]

Something seems to be happening.

TALA: I think they must have risen.

ROLFE: Who?

TALA: The Cardinal-Compromissaries.

ROLFE: Will they have reached a decision?

TALA: We shall soon see. Here they come.

[*The nine* CARDINAL-COMPROMISSARIES, *in full purple, led by the* CARDINAL ARCHDEACON, *proceed slowly on stage, bow to the altar, then turn inwards to face* ROLFE *and* TALACRYN.

If possible, OTHER MEMBERS OF THE SACRED COLLEGE, MASTERS OF CEREMONIES, NOBLEMEN, HIGH PAPAL OFFICIALS, SWISS GUARDS, *should crowd on too. As soon as all are on stage, the bell ceases to clang.*]

ROLFE [*in whisper to* TALACRYN]: As well try to divine the thoughts of an unworn shoe, as read the face of a Cardinal.

TALA: Sssh!

[*Now distantly the Litany begins again, chanted back and forth in tenor voices.*]

ROLFE [*in whisper to* TALACRYN]: What is it? What is happening?

TALA: I think God has given us a Pope.

ROLFE: Whom?

[TALACRYN *puts his fingers to his lips.*
Now the Litany ceases and all turn inwards.]

CARDINAL ARCHDEACON: Reverend Lord, the Sacred College has elected thee to be the successor to St Peter. Wilt thou accept pontificality?

[*Since all present are now facing towards* ROLFE *and* TALACRYN, ROLFE *assumes it is the latter who is being addressed. He turns towards* TALACRYN *with a happy smile but sees that he is now kneeling. Confused, he turns back to look at the* CARDINAL ARCHDEACON.]

CARDINAL ARCHDEACON [*with greater emphasis*]: Reverend Lord, the Sacred College has elected thee to be the successor of St Peter. Wilt thou accept pontificality?

[*Another pause.*
ROLFE, *looking round to where all are on their knees facing inwards towards him, at last realizes that the awful question is addressed to him.*]

ROLFE: *Reverend* Lord? Will *I*?

TALA [*whisper*]: The response is '*Volo*' – or '*Nolo*'.
[ROLFE *takes a deep breath, crossing right hand over left on his breast.*]

ROLFE: *Volo* . . . I will.

All kneel as a CHAMBERLAIN, *bearing the Triple Tiara, advances towards* ROLFE.

CURTAIN

ACT TWO

Scene One

MRS CROWE's *parlour in London. Seated is* JEREMIAH SANT, F.R.S. (*Fellowship of Religious Segregation, an extremist group, out-lawed in Ulster, dedicated to the persecution of Roman Catholics in general and the Pope in particular*). *He is a journalist by profession and a street corner rabble-rousing politician who does not stop at violence. A dangerous fanatic.*

SANT *and* MRS CROWE *are seated together on the sofa enjoying stiff drinks and a newspaper which* SANT *reads aloud.*

SANT: Here, listen to this . . . '. . . and as representatives of the Catholic world looked on, the triple crown was placed on the head of the first English Pope to ascend the throne of St Peter since Nicholas Breakspeare became Pope Hadrian IV in 1154.' [*He interrupts himself.*] Begod, doesn't it make you want to puke to think of an Englishman sinking so low.

MRS CROWE: What's so special about it, Jerry? I can't see why you get so excited about it.

SANT: Get so excited about it? Rome rule means Home Rule, doesn't it?

SANT: But I'm thinking maybe the Papishes have cooked their own goose this time.

MRS CROWE: How's that then?

SANT: Well, for one thing, it will queer the pitch of the Home Rulers. One false move and it could be civil war in Ireland with the Fenians cutting each other's dirty throats. They'll not stand for an Englishman giving out the orders, Pope or no.

MRS CROWE: Oh, I'll never understand Irish politics as long as I live. . . . Here, let me fill your glass.

37

SANT: Aye. You do that, sweetheart.

[*Pause.* SANT *has now blown off most of his steam.*]

MRS CROWE [*filling both glasses*]: Looking after men: that's something I do understand.

SANT: True for you, Nancy. Never a truer word. Slainte!

MRS CROWE: Here's cheers! [*She comes and sits beside him.*]

SANT: But there's one thing I've never been able to figure out – what you see in that abomination of desolation.

MRS CROWE: Who?

SANT: Rolfe.

MRS CROWE: What *I* see in *him*? Oh, please, Jerry. Give me a little credit. Do you know what he used to do? – No, I don't want to talk about it. I can't bear to speak about him any more. [*She starts to snivel.*]

SANT: Now just a moment, Nancy. Just a moment . . . Here, give us your glass.

MRS CROWE [*upset*]: Oh, no thank you, Jerry.

SANT: Come on, sweetheart. Just a half'un.

MRS CROWE: Oh well, all right then.

[*He fills both glasses generously. They drink and* MRS CROWE *makes a face.*]

MRS CROWE: Ooh, this is strong. [*She downs it in one, nevertheless.*]

SANT: Never mind. It'll do you good. Now, Nance, just now you started to say something and bye and bye you're going to finish it. But first I'm going to tell you one or two things.

MRS CROWE: What things?

SANT: Well, first, how would you like to come on a wee trip with me to Rome?

MRS CROWE: To Rome? But, Jerry, how could I? I mean . . .

SANT: Oh, don't you worry about that. We'll be properly chaperoned I promise you.

MRS CROWE: But I've got nothing to wear.

SANT: No problem at all. Now just listen to me. The Fellowship of Religious Segregation of which, as you may know,

I'm a Senior Brother, are very disturbed by certain recent events and, as loyal servants of the Crown, we feel it our duty to do whatever we can to protect the Free Churches of the United Kingdom. [*He gets up and postures round the room.*]

MRS CROWE: Yes, Jerry, but what's this all to do with you and me going to Rome?

SANT: I'll tell ye in a minute. Now the F.R.S. are sending a deputation to the Vatican to demand certain safeguards for Protestants in the light of the aforesaid recent events, and I'm heading that deputation. 'Sing and rejoice, O daughter of Zion: for, lo, I come, and I will dwell in the midst of thee, saith the Lord'.

MRS CROWE [*impressed*]: Oh, I say.

SANT: Now, you'll be asking yourself – and rightly – why I'm inviting you to come with me, and I wouldn't insult your intelligence by trying to pretend that it was just for business reasons only . . . Here, where's your glass? [*He fills their two glasses again.*]

MRS CROWE: Not another.

[SANT *refills both glasses and* MRS CROWE *accepts without further demur.*]

SANT: . . . besides, I think I can say, Nance, that we know one another too well for that.

MRS CROWE: Oh, it is nice to see you back again, Jerry, I must say. Things have not been too easy for me lately, one way and another.

SANT: Aye. I suspected as much when I came. And I wouldn't be surprised if it were something to do with that agent of the Whore of Babylon, the erstwhile Baron Corvo. Eh?

[MRS CROWE *doesn't reply but consoles herself with another drink.*]

I'm right, Nancy, aren't I?

[MRS CROWE *nods her head.*]

That little barmstick! And I'll wager he hasn't paid you the rent – sneaking out of the house the way he did.

MRS CROWE [*getting maudlin*]: And not even a line to say that he'd got there safely . . . not even a postcard. [*Starts to snivel.*]

SANT: Aye. Well we'll soon even with him. [*He crosses and sits beside her, putting an arm round her shoulder.*] Now a little earlier you were going to tell me something. Now's the time. Come on, Nance.

MRS CROWE: No, I couldn't, Jerry. [*Snivels.*]

SANT [*getting tough*]: Now, Nancy, you can and you shall tell me.

MRS CROWE [*content that the moment has come to give in*]: Oh, Jerry, it's been going on for years. He – he wouldn't leave me alone, never. He was always – always trying to – to interfere with me, even when Mr Crowe was alive. I've had no peace whatever whenever he was around, Jerry, and I – I just couldn't keep him away. [*She turns and buries her head in* SANT's *shoulder, sobbing.*]

SANT [*surprised*]: Well I'll be damned!

MRS CROWE: Well don't sound so surprised. Aren't I attractive any more?

SANT: No, no. Of course you are, sweetheart. It's just that I always thought . . . Anyway, no Papish traitor shall defile with his dirty touch a respectable Protestant lady and get away with it. He shall pay right dearly for this or my name's not Jeremiah Sant.

MRS CROWE [*quietly and viciously*]: Make him squirm, Jerry. Make him squirm.

SANT *kisses her violently on the mouth.*

BLACKOUT

Scene Two

An Audience Chamber in the Vatican. The Pontifical Throne is unoccupied.

Three princes of the Church enter and perambulate. They are CARDINAL RAGNA, *the Secretary of State* (*elderly, bull-like, aggressive, Italian*), CARDINAL BERSTEIN (*cold, arrogant, German*) *and* FATHER ST ALBANS (*Prepositor-General of Jesuits, the truculent 'Black Pope', English.*)

ST ALBANS: To a great extent I blame myself. I should have known what a formidable politician my compatriot, Cardinal Courtleigh, was. When it became apparent that Your Lordship's [*inclines towards* RAGNA] candidature was being blocked by the French and Iberian faction, [RAGNA *makes a gesture of disgust*] you should have pressed for old Gentilotto.

BERSTEIN: Gentilotto would have been good. An old man but a good man. He would have been no trouble.

ST ALBANS: I had no idea that he had in mind this parvenu.

RAGNA: Parvenu, si.

ST ALBANS: Still less that he could have succeeded in foisting him on all nine of you!

BERSTEIN: A man of such humility, he said. Huh! Humility!

ST ALBANS: He has the humility of an Old Testament prophet.

BERSTEIN: Ja. He is not a humble man.

RAGNA: And you saw also the business of the Pontifical ring! Why he must insist to have amethyst ring? The late Holiness take always the emerald ring. But no; the ceremony of Consecration is delayed one half-hour to find amethyst ring. Who does he think he is this man?

ST ALBANS: I think he thinks he's Pope – with some justification, of course.

RAGNA [*disgust*]: Eh! 'He, who was a frog, is now a king.'

BERSTEIN: 'He who is born of a hen always scratches the ground.'

RAGNA: *Sí. È vero!* And when the Cardinal Archdeacon say 'Holiness, what is the Pontifical name you will choose?' He say 'Hadrian the Seventh'. I said to him – you heard me, no? – 'Your Holiness would perhaps prefer to be called Leo, or Pius, or Gregory, as is the modern manner.' But he say –

ST ALBANS [*imitating* ROLFE]: – 'The first and previous English Pontiff was Hadrian the Fourth: the second and present English Pontiff is Hadrian the Seventh. It pleases Us; and so, by Our Own impulse, We command.'

RAGNA [*in disgust*]: 'By Our Own impulse We command.' Such arrogance!

RAGNA: Eh! But you heard what He said to me when I tell him it is very pericoloso –

ST ALBANS: – dangerous.

RAGNA: – dangerous to walk to Lateran?

ST ALBANS: My Lord Berstein and I were somewhat distant from Your Lordship at the time.

RAGNA: I said for the Holy Father to walk to Lateran through streets of Rome today is madness. The city is full of Jews and Freemasons. It is suicide for You, I say, and is murder for me.

ST ALBANS: And what did he say?

RAGNA: He say 'good, the Church is badly wanting a new martyr'.

[ST ALBANS *suppresses laughter.* BERSTEIN *tut-tuts.*

OTHER MEMBERS OF SACRED COLLEGE *enter. They number as many as possible. The Pontifical Throne remains vacant.*

[*Enter* COURTLEIGH, *wheeled in bathchair.*]

COURT: Can anyone enlighten me as to the reason for this hasty summons?

RAGNA [*with gesture of resignation*]: *Ecco!*

COURT: Had to gobble me breakfast. Haven't even had a chance to read *The Times.*

ST ALBANS: Your Eminence could hardly have done so.

COURT: What do you mean?

ST ALBANS: I am informed that an embargo has been placed on all newspapers within the Vatican.

COURT: Extraordinary . . . !

ST ALBANS: . . . however, I made it my business to find out the reason for this and it appears that the embargo was placed by His Holiness prior to the publication of his Bull and Breve,

[*Exclamations of amazement from several* CARDINALS.]

. . . further, I made it my business to obtain a copy of the text of this Bull and I think Your Emininences will be interested if I read it to you,

[*More exclamations.*

ST ALBANS *clears his throat and pauses for effect. He then reads from a sheet of paper.*

The CARDINALS *stop muttering.*]

We, Hadrian the Seventh, Vicar of Christ, Servant of the servants of God, speak thus: We find Ourselves the sovereign of an estate to which We hold no title deeds. But Our Kingdom is not of this world. So, therefore, We, Vicar of Christ, Successor to The Throne of St Peter, do now make Our formal and unconditional renunciation to temporal sovereignty.

[CARDINALS *gasp.*]

Our predecessors followed other counsels and they acted in the knowledge of their responsibility to God. We, on Our part, act as We deem best. We are God's vice-gerent and this is Our will. [*Quickly.*] Given at Rome, at St Peter's by the Vatican, on this day of Our Supreme Pontificate.

[*There is a moment of utter silence, then:*]

RAGNA [*shouting*]: Judas! Judas! This shall not be!

ST ALBANS: Unfortunately, Lord Cardinal, it can be – and it is.

RAGNA: Am I Secretary of State or am I not Secretary of State? I am asking your Eminences. If the Pontiff is no longer

43

temporal sovereign, how am I Secretary of the Vatican State? You tell me I am to be dismissed by this – this clerk who has the sack from two – not one – but two – ecclesiastical colleges?

BERSTEIN: Two colleges! [*Tut-tuts.*]

TALA: His Holiness believes the world is sick for want of the Church. He believes, I think, that we should turn all our efforts and attention to the pursuit of non-secular matters.

RAGNA: *Va bene, va bene.* But I tell you His Holiness has very special conception of His Apostolic character. He think that is enough. It is not enough.

BERSTEIN: *Ja, ja.* It is not enough. If the Temporal power is worth having, it is worth fighting for.

ST ALBANS: I do not say that I disagree with Your Eminence.

RAGNA: Then perhaps you will make a suggestion. You say Jesuits are always very clever. Why do you not suggest we convene the Oecumenical Council? Eh?

BERSTEIN: *Ja, ja.* The Oecumenical Council only can deal with such matters.

RAGNA: I say this man is a heretic. I say he is the Anti-Pope. And I say the Sacred College must act now – before it is too late.

ST ALBANS: And I wouldn't necessarily argue with your Eminence, but the Oecumenical Council of the Vatican has stood adjourned since – I think I am right in saying – since 1870. All the same –

RAGNA: But all the same it can be re-convened, no?

BERSTEIN: Under the circumstances it is the only thing to do. With that I agree.

ST ALBANS: If the Sacred College should choose to demand –

RAGNA [*roaring*]: The Sacred College *should* demand.

[*Unnoticed,* HADRIAN *comes quietly on stage. For the first time he is seen wearing the white garments of a Pope.*]

If there's any anxiety or doubt in any minds the Sacred College *must* demand.

44

HADRIAN [*very quietly*]: Pray, what must the Sacred College demand, Lord Cardinal?

[*All react at the sudden appearance of the Pope.* RAGNA, *taken off guard, can only work his jaw defiantly.* HADRIAN *persists in his most ominously gentle voice.*]

Your Eminence is free to address Us.

RAGNA [*recovering his truculence slightly*]: I wish rather to address the Sacred College.

HADRIAN [*sweetly*]: You have Our permission to do so. [*He looks round the room noting the reactions of those present.*]

RAGNA: I wish to – [*Clears his throat to gain time.*] I wish to –

HADRIAN: You wish to denounce Us as Heretic and Pseudo-pontiff. And, to do so, you wish to convene an Oecumenical Council. Is that not correct?

[RAGNA, *his own words taken from his mouth, remains silent. His face working.*]

That generally is done by oblique-eyed cardinals who cannot accustom themselves to new pontiffs. But Lord Cardinals, if such an idea should be presented to you, be ye mindful that none but the Supreme Pontiff can convoke an Oecumenical Council, and that the decrees of such are ineffective without the express sanction of the Supreme Pontiff. We are conscious of your love and of your loathing of Our Person and Our Acts. We value the one and regret the other. But ye voluntarily have sworn obedience to Us, and We claim it. Nothing must and nothing shall obstruct Us. Let that be known.

Wherefore, Most Eminent Lords and Venerable Fathers, let not the sheep of Christ's flock be neglected while the shepherds exchange anathemas. Try, Venerable Fathers, to believe that the time has come for taking stock. Ask yourselves whether we really are as successful as we think we are – whether in fact we are not abject and lamentable failures in the eyes of God. We have added and added to the riches, pomp and power of the Church yet everywhere there is great wealth alongside dire poverty; there are strong nations brutally holding small ones in slavery; above all there are millions of people of goodwill looking to us for moral and spiritual leadership who get from us only dogmatic interpretation of Canon Law in return. If then we have so far failed in spreading Christ's Gospel, let us try anew. Let us try the road of Apostolic simplicity – the simplicity of Peter the Fisherman. At least let us try.

[*There is a total silence.*]

Your Eminences have permission to retire.

[*For a moment there is silence. Then* TALACRYN *goes quickly to re-affirm his allegiance by kissing the Pontifical ring. Then hesitantly at first, the others follow.* RAGNA, *still recalcitrant, makes the briefest possible acknowledgement.* COURTLEIGH *in bathchair is last to leave. Having made obeisance the other Prelates file severally off stage murmuring among themselves.* HADRIAN *and* COURTLEIGH *remain upstage.*]

BERSTEIN [*murmuring*]: His Holiness has averted a schism.

HADRIAN [*to* COURT]: We should be glad if your Eminence could spare a few moments longer of your time.

COURT [*coolly*]: I am at Your Holiness's disposal.

[*The* CARDINALS *filter off stage.*]

I pray Your Holiness will forgive this chair.

HADRIAN: We trust Your Eminence is not seriously incommoded.

COURT: A very English complaint, Holy Father, a touch of the gout.

HADRIAN: Accept Our sympathy for your English complaint. We too have them, but of a different nature. We desire to establish relations with Your Eminence, chiefly because you hold so responsible a position in England, a country dear above all others to Us.

[COURTLEIGH *puts on his Cardinalatial Mask expressive of the old and wise condescending to give ear to the young and rash.*]

COURT: Proceed, Most Holy Father.

46

HADRIAN: It is Our wish to make England's people prepared for the Lord. But We find Ourselves impeded at the outset by the present conduct of the English Roman Catholics – especially of the aboriginal English Catholics.

[COURTLEIGH *reacts sharply then bows slightly and continues to attend.* HADRIAN *picks up a bunch of press cuttings.*]

Kindly give Us your opnion of this statement, Eminence. I quote from a London newspaper whose views are not necessarily my own. 'The Roman Catholic laity resident in England are asking Parliament to set up some control over Roman Catholic monies and interests. It is alleged that no account is afforded by the Roman Catholic Bishops of the management or disbursements of such properties and monies ...' Well?

COURT: The scandal emanated from a priest of my Archdiocese, Holiness. We were successful in preventing it from spreading.

HADRIAN: Oh! Then there was such a petition? I was prepared to ascribe it to the imagination of one of the bright young men usually employed by the monstrous old proprietor of this newspaper. And were there many supporters of the petition?

COURT [*raising hand*]: Unfortunately, there were a number.

HADRIAN: And were there any grounds for the allegations?

COURT: Holy Father, we cannot be expected to account to every Tom, Dick and Harry for the hundreds of bequests and endowments which we administer.

HADRIAN: Why not, if your accounts are properly audited? We assume they are?

COURT: Ah – to a great extent, yes.

HADRIAN: To a great extent? Not invariably? But do you really consider your clergy capable of financial administration?

COURT: As capable as other men.

HADRIAN: Priests are not 'as other men'.

COURT: But what would Your Holiness have?

HADRIAN: We entirely disapprove of the clergy using any secular power whatever, especially such power as inheres in the command of money. The clergy are ministers – ministers – not masters. The clergy are *more*, not *less* human, and they certainly are not the pick of humanity.

COURT: Even if I were to agree, I still do not precisely see Your Holiness's point.

HADRIAN: No? Then let us take another. [*He takes a small green ticket from among his papers.*] This comes from your Eminence's archdiocese: 'Church of the Sacred Heart – admit bearer to Midnight Mass – Christmas Eve – Middle seat 1/6d.' Surely not some form of discrimination?

[COURTLEIGH *looks at the card as though it were of no significance.*]

COURT [*shrugging*]: A small attempt to prevent – ah – improper persons from attending these services.

HADRIAN: But 'improper' persons should be encouraged to attend.

COURT [*irritated*]: And have scenes of disorder and profanation?

HADRIAN: We are determined that our Churches be made as free to the lost as to the saved.

COURT: May I be permitted to ask what experience Your Holiness has had in parochial administration?

HADRIAN: You could answer that question yourself, your Eminence. But I've attended many midnight masses and heard no sign of the profanation of which you speak. Sots and harlots were undoubtedly present but they were not disorderly. They were cowed, they were sleepy, they were curious, but they made no noise. If means of grace are obtainable in a church, who dare deny them to those who need them most. You are here to serve – and only to serve. We especially disapprove of any system which makes access to the church difficult – like this admission fee.

COURT: Holy Father, the clergy must live.

HADRIAN: And so they shall. But pew-rents are abominable –
and so are pews. Abolish them both.

COURT [*beside himself with rage*]: Your Holiness speaks as
though he was not one of us.

[HADRIAN *pauses and fixes the* CARDINAL *with a look.*]

HADRIAN: Look at your Catholic Directory and see the
advertisement of A Priest who is prepared to pay bank
interest on investments – in plain words, to be a money
lender in direct contravention to St Luke. Look at the
Catholic Hour and see the advertisement of a Priest who
actually trades as a tobacconist. Look in the precincts of your
churches and see the tables of the Fenian literature sellers and
the seats of them that sell tickets for stage plays and bazaars –
No, my Lord Cardinal, the clergy attempt too much. They
may be excellent priests but as tradesmen, stock-jobbers and
variety entertainers, they are catastrophes.

COURT [*with resignation*]: But Holy Father, do think for a
moment. What are the clergy to live on?

HADRIAN: The free-will offerings of the faithful.

COURT: But suppose the faithful do not give of their free will?

HADRIAN: Then starve and go to heaven.

COURT [*stung once more to defend himself*]: Your Holiness will
permit me to remind you that I, myself, was consecrated
Bishop fourteen years before You were made a Christian at
baptism. It seems to me that You should give Your seniors
credit for having consciences of their own.

HADRIAN: My dear Lord Cardinal, if We had seen the least
sign of the said consciences –

COURT: I am not the only member of the Sacred College who
thinks that Your Holiness's attitude partakes of – shall I say
singularity – and – ah – arrogance.

HADRIAN: Singularity? Oh, We sincerely hope so. But arrogance – We cannot call it arrogance that We have at-
tempted to show you something of Our frame of mind.

COURT: What then, Holy Father, would You wish me to do?

HADRIAN: We wish you to act upon the sum of Our words and conduct in order that England may have a good, and not a bad, example from English Catholics. No more than that. The Barque of Peter is way off course. Lord Cardinal, can the new captain count on the loyal support of His lieutenant in trying to bring her head round?

COURT [*makes an immense effort*]: Holy Father, I assure you that You may count on me.

HADRIAN: We realize the immense effort on Your part that has made you give Us this assurance and it gladdens Us to see this evidence of the Grace of your Divine Vocation.

[COURTLEIGH *bows slightly*.]

Well now, Lord Cardinal, to change the metaphor, let us put away the flail and take up the crook. [*He sweeps his documents, press cuttings, etc., into a folder and puts it away in his desk.*] So shall we take a little stroll in the garden and say some Office?

COURT [*surprised*]: Oh, well certainly, with pleasure – that is if Your Holiness doesn't mind walking by the side of my bathchair, that is . . .

HADRIAN: Oh, but We do. It is Our invariable custom to walk *behind* bathchairs and push them.

COURT: Oh but, Holiness, I could not for one moment permit –

HADRIAN: No, but for just one hour you will submit.

COURT: But, Holy Father, really –

HADRIAN: Nonsense, man, do you suppose that One has never pushed a bathchair before?

COURT: All the same, Holiness, it is hardly –

HADRIAN: Now sit quietly and open your breviary and start reading the office.

[COURTLEIGH *obeys*.]

We will look over your shoulder and make the responses. [*He swivels the* CARDINAL'*s bathchair around*.] It's awfully good exercise, you know.

ACT TWO, SCENE TWO

[*Respectively saying and responding to the Office of the Day, the* POPE *pushes the aged* CARDINAL *off the stage.*

The lights change and come up on SANT *and* MRS CROWE *in Rome. They are seated at a café table out of doors.* MRS CROWE *shields herself from the sun with a parasol and* SANT *fans himself with a Panama hat. He holds a piece of paper in his other hand.*]

SANT: This is my ultimatum. Listen. [*Reads.*] 'Since my earlier communication in which I had the pleasure of addressing you on the aims of the Fellowship of Religious Segregation, I have been anxiously waiting the favour of an acknowledgement of same. In case the subject has slipped your memory, I should remind you that we were not adverse to give our careful consideration to any proposal you may see fit to make, financial or otherwise,' [*Aside.*] – that's putting it fair and square, eh?

MRS CROWE: Yes, Jerry, but how's he going to know that you want to talk to him about the other – you know ...

SANT: Hold your horses. I haven't come to the guts of it yet. [*Continues.*] 'But I am quite at a loss to understand on what grounds you have not yet favoured me with a reply unless there is anything on which you would like further explanation. In which case, I will be most happy to call on you per appointment for which I have been waiting at the above address here in Rome for some weeks and neglecting my business at considerable expense and inconvenience which a man in my position cannot be expected to incur and common courtesy demands should be made good.'

[*This side of stage now blacks out.*

The other side with TALACRYN *reading aloud to* HADRIAN *lights up.* HADRIAN *sits still and tense, puffing furiously at the home-rolled fag in his mouth.*]

TALA [*reading*]: 'I therefore trust that in view of the not altogether pleasant facts that are in the possession of myself and another party well-known to yourself, you will see fit to accord me a private interview at your earliest convenience. Hoping that I will not . . .

HADRIAN: Stop! I cannot bring myself to hear any more of that illiterate filth.

[*He remains rigid. His hand trembles as he removes his cigarette.*]

TALA: Forgive the presumption, but Your Holiness seems unduly upset by this impertinent nonsense.

HADRIAN: It is not His Holiness who is upset, but Frederick William Rolfe.

TALA: Again forgive the presumption, but one has known Your Holiness for some years. Who are these enemies, Holy Father?

HADRIAN: Prurient scum. Pithycanthropoids and Neanderthals who beset Our path in Our previous and ghastly existence. Worms who turn to traduce Us.

TALA: They can be annihilated, Holiness. Surely some guillotine can be brought down that would effectively silence these – these –

HADRIAN: Blackmailers? Since Our conscience is clear, We have no desire to be so dynamic. We would not touch ordure even with a shovel.

TALA: But silence is more likely to inflame such people than to quiet them. Supposing in their frustration they go to the newspapers.

HADRIAN: Then, doubtless, the Sacred College will erect their tailfeathers and gobble like a flock of huge turkey-cocks: 'Behold the Anti-Pope!' they will say, and glare whole Inquisitions at Us.

TALA: Respectfully, Holiness, the matter should not be allowed to reach such a pass. As Your Holiness rightly assumes, those within the Sacred College who were against Your accession would welcome a scandal directed at Your Person.

HADRIAN: Let them have a scandal. Let them keep aloof in their vermilion sulks. It is not Our will to move in this matter.

TALA: But, forgive me if I persist, Holiness –

HADRIAN [*sharply*]: Do not persist. [*Changing from the pontifical to the familiar.*] Tell me, Frank, what have you been doing today?

TALA: Today? Oh, I paid a visit, as a matter of fact, to your old college.

HADRIAN [*freezing*]: Oh?

TALA: They cannot understand why You have not yet been to see them.

HADRIAN: Is not the Rector still the same man who once expelled me – brutally and without explanation?

TALA: The Rector is an old man now, sensible to the errors of his youth, as we all are.

HADRIAN [*to himself*]: The wound goes deep. It has never properly healed.

TALA: Perhaps this is the moment for cauterizing the wound, Holiness. Strangely, I forgot the horrors of my own times there after I'd visited them once or twice. Besides, the young men love to see one and the older men – the principals – like to see vermilion take note of them.

HADRIAN [*suddenly getting up*]: Frank, let's go to the College now. We can get there in time for lunch.

TALA [*looking pleased*]: What a good idea.

Scene Three

St. Andrew's College, Rome.

We hear a distant bell. A distant Litany. Some young SEMINAR-ISTS *pass by in purple sopranos, singing. Among them we see* ROSE. HADRIAN *enters with* TALACRYN *and the* RECTOR. *The latter dressed in black, is an old man whose behaviour before the* POPE *is a mixture of self-importance and obsequiousness – the Headmaster humouring a distinguished parent.*

RECTOR: This has been a great day for the College, Holy Father.

    [HADRIAN *ignores the flattery.*]

    Of course, had we known that Your Holiness intended to honour us, a proper reception –

HADRIAN: Quite unnecessary. Our children expect to see Us and We came to be seen. We now wish to know something of one student in particular.

RECTOR: Who is that, Holy Father?

HADRIAN: The somewhat older man who looks so hungry and took only bread and water at luncheon.

RECTOR: Ah, poor fellow!

HADRIAN: Now, why do you say that, Monsignore?

RECTOR: Well Holiness, I'm afraid this is not the place for him. He's very sensitive and doesn't really get on with the others.

HADRIAN: Does he quarrel with them?

RECTOR: Oh no. But he takes pains to avoid them.

HADRIAN: Perhaps he has his reasons.

RECTOR: Perhaps, but his attitude does not seem suitable in one hoping to attain Orders! He is not what I would call a good mixer.

HADRIAN: You talk as if he aspired to be a sporting parson.

RECTOR [*nettled*]: I must tell Your Holiness that I do not feel that he has a real Vocation for the priesthood.

HADRIAN: Please know, Monsignore, that We have not come

54

here to brag or to gloat, but We feel bound to remind you that your judgement as to vocation has, in the past, been in error.

RECTOR [*shaken*]: I am only too mindful – Your Holiness's personal case has for a long time been – it was a long time ago. I can only say in extenuation that to err is human.

HADRIAN: Human error is sometimes excusable. *In*-human behaviour is not. Ill-considered judgements by those in authority are damnably culpable.

[*The* RECTOR *winces.*]

What is the name of this student who has 'no vocation'?

RECTOR: Rose, Holiness. George Arthur Rose.

HADRIAN: We wish to speak to him.

RECTOR: If it pleases Your Holiness.

HADRIAN: We will speak to him alone.

[*The* RECTOR *bows and leaves.*]

HADRIAN [*to* TALACRYN *as soon as the* RECTOR *has left*]: Were We too severe, Frank? The wish to smoke has made Us irritable.

TALA [*smiling*]: Your Holiness was altogether admirable. I must admit to having enjoyed the last five minutes more than a Christian should.

HADRIAN [*looking round and sniffing*]: Still the same smell: boiled mutton-fat and hot boy.

TALA: They seem to be the inescapable adjuncts of education.

HADRIAN: Inescapable? Nonsense! We have half a mind to appoint you Protector of this College. Yes, that's right. A Celtic Protector for a Celtic College. Good. We shall give you a breve as soon as We get back to Vatican. You will give them sanitation – and sanity, for goodness sake. You might make that shrubbery into a gymnasium. And what about a swimming-pool . . . with a lovely terrace on the top?

TALA: I don't see why not.

HADRIAN: And, Frank, make friends with them and see what

you can do to take that horrible secretive suppressed look out of their young eyes. You understand?

TALA: I think so, Holiness.

[*The* RECTOR *arrives with* ROSE *dressed in the violet cassock and black soprano of a seminarist.*]

RECTOR: Mr Rose, Your Holiness.

[ROSE *observes the forms.*]

HADRIAN [*to* RECTOR]: You will be pleased to hear, Monsignore, that We have appointed Cardinal Talacryn Protector of St Andrew's College. His Eminence would be most grateful if you would now take him on a detailed tour of the kitchens and sanitary arrangements.

[*The* RECTOR *looks surprised but is now totally submissive.*]

RECTOR: As Your Holiness pleases.

[*The* RECTOR *and* TALACRYN *withdraw.* ROSE *does not show surprise but stands with dignity and reserve.*]

HADRIAN: Dear Son, on slight knowledge We have the impression you are one of the unhappy ones. Will you confide in Us.

ROSE: Sanctity, I have not complained.

HADRIAN: But now you may do so.

ROSE: I have no reason – I do not wish to do so.

HADRIAN: How old are you, my son?

ROSE: Sanctity, twenty-nine.

HADRIAN: And you find your environment disagreeable?

ROSE: All environments are more or less disagreeable to me.

HADRIAN: Up to the present at least. You find that your circumstances prevent you from doing yourself justice here?

ROSE: That may be my fault.

HADRIAN: They mock you, no doubt.

ROSE: I suppose that is the case, Holiness.

HADRIAN: So was Jesus Christ mocked. But why are you?

ROSE: Because for my ablutions I carry two cans of water up two hundred and two steps every day.

HADRIAN: No doubt they say you must be a very unclean person to need so much washing.

ROSE: Sanctity, you are quoting the Rector. How does Your Holiness know so exactly?

HADRIAN [*laughing*]: Have they ever put a snake in your watercans?

ROSE: No, they have not done that.

HADRIAN: They did in Ours. Isn't it absurd?

ROSE: It is – and very disconcerting.

HADRIAN: But you try not to let it disconcert you?

ROSE: I try but I fail. My heart is always on my sleeve and the daws peck it. So I try to protect myself in isolation.

HADRIAN: That they call 'sulkiness'!

ROSE: Yes. Your Holiness knows so exactly –

HADRIAN [*almost to himself*]: We also were never able to arrange to be loved. Do you always live on bread and water?

ROSE: Yes, except for eggs.

HADRIAN: Why?

ROSE: I have been into the kitchen and seen – things. They cannot deposit sputum inside the shells of boiled eggs.

HADRIAN: Do you like bread and water?

ROSE: No. But in order not to be singular I eat and drink what I can of what is set before me. But because of that, I am deemed more singular than ever.

HADRIAN: Yet you choose to persevere, my Son!

ROSE: Sanctity, I must. I am called.

HADRIAN: You are sure of that?

ROSE: It is the only thing in all the world of which I am sure.

HADRIAN: Yet you know that this college is not the place for you?

ROSE: I suppose not. But my diocesan sent me here and I intend to serve my sentence.

HADRIAN: Dear Son, what is your ambition?

ROSE: Priesthood.

HADRIAN: And you will persevere – for however long?

ROSE: For twenty years if need be.

HADRIAN: We persevered for just that length of time.

ROSE: Then so will I.

HADRIAN: My Son, it is in Our power to grant you a favour. Do you wish to ask Us for anything?

ROSE: No thank you, Sanctity.

HADRIAN: Is there nothing We can do for you?

ROSE: Nothing, Sanctity.

HADRIAN: My Son, do you think you are ready for priesthood?

ROSE: I am ready as soon as I may be summoned, Sanctity.

HADRIAN: You shall be summoned. Come to Vatican tomorrow and ask for Cardinal Talacryn. He will expect you.
  [HADRIAN *rises*.]
Your desire may soon be fulfilled. Will you pray for Us, dear Son?

ROSE: Holy Father, I most surely will.

HADRIAN: Good-bye and God bless you.
  [ROSE *kneels and* HADRIAN *gives blessing.* ROSE *goes.* TALACRYN *re-enters.*]

HADRIAN [*to* TALA]: What a delicious day it has been, Frank. You persuaded Us and We are grateful.

TALA: I think the walk did Your Holiness good.

HADRIAN: It was not just the walk, but something quite other – as though a curtain has been lifted or, more exactly, as if We had been given a brief glimpse into a human heart.

TALA: This is a rare and wonderful experience, Holiness.

HADRIAN: Rare? You are Our confessor. You must know that for Us the experience is unique. Frank, We have just had the first feeling of undiluted enjoyment of human society which We can ever remember.

TALA: Do you remember what I said to you in London, Holiness? I said that if You could find it in Yourself to love your neighbour it would lead You to love God.

HADRIAN: Love ... yes ... We have recognized for the first time in Ourselves a new and unborn power, a perfectly

strange capability. Today We have made experience of a
feeling which – well, which We suppose – at any rate will
pass for – Love.

Scene Four

An Anteroom in the Vatican.
Lights come up on AGNES, *Hadrian's former char. She sits on a chair looking very nervous.* FR ROSE, *now in the cassock of an ordained priest, enters.*

FR ROSE: Mrs Dixon?

AGNES: Yers?

FR ROSE: His Holiness asked me to convey his apologies to you. He has been slightly delayed.

AGNES: That's quite all right, dear, ta.

[FR ROSE *nods. There is an awkward silence as they both wait for* HADRIAN.]

AGNES: Been keeping busy then?

FR ROSE [*slightly taken aback*]: Well as private chaplain to his Holiness I find the days full.

AGNES: I dare say you do. He's a handful all right. I used to look after him myself.

[*Further conversation is prevented by the entrance of* HADRIAN.]

FR ROSE: Mrs Agnes Dixon, Your Holiness.

[AGNES *trots across and flops on her knees.* HADRIAN *immediately attempts to assist her to rise.*]

HADRIAN: Agnes.

AGNES: Oooh, my joints!

HADRIAN [*throwing off completely his cold, pontifical manner*]: Agnes, please sit down.

AGNES: I don't mind, sir.

HADRIAN: Please, Agnes, here. [*He assists her to a chair.*]

AGNES [*sitting*]: Ooh, that's better. I've been on my feet all day and don't these marble floors tell.

HADRIAN: I'm so sorry, Agnes.

AGNES: I shouldn't be saying such things, should I, not now with you living here.

60

HADRIAN: Good friends are few, Agnes – particularly in the Vatican.

AGNES: These your chairs, are they?

HADRIAN: Well, I suppose they go with the job.

AGNES: Not very comfy, are they? Still ... Oh, there I am again! But, there, I can't help but think of you still as Mr Rolfe I used to do for.

HADRIAN: It's good to hear you say so, Agnes.

AGNES [scrabbling in a capacious bag and eventually bringing forth a packet]: Here we are, then.

HADRIAN [taking it]: What is this?

AGNES: Why, the change, of course.

HADRIAN: Change?

AGNES: From the money you sent me to buy that house. I got it cheaper than we thought because it'd been empty so long.

HADRIAN: Oh, but you dear good soul, I didn't expect any change. It's all yours. Besides, you may need it to tide you over till you get the lodgers?

AGNES: Till I can get the lodgers? Why, I'm turning them away already.

HADRIAN: Good, well bank it for the winter. Do you remember cooking two dinners one Christmas Day? One was ate. The other you carried to some fellow who was out of work. I remember because you spilt gravy on your frock and hoped I hadn't seen.

AGNES: No one can't say you haven't got a long memory. Can they?

HADRIAN: You stinted yourself then, Agnes. Now don't stint yourself any more. Give away as many hot dinners as you please.

AGNES: Well, I'm one of the lucky ones, I reckon. It's not easy for some nowadays, particularly the old 'uns what have no family ... [She dives in her bag again.] I nearly forgot, what with all the excitement and walking along those stone corridors with those gentlemen in their fancy get-up. One of them was ever so stuck-up, he was. I couldn't help saying, 'I seen plenty more like you, my lad, at the old Holborn Empire'. Oh yes, I did, but I don't think he knew what I meant. There, I knew I had it somewhere. [*She produces a jar of pickles.*] It's the pickles you always had a fancy for. Made just the same as I used to. You always had a tooth for them, didn't you?

HADRIAN: Dear, good Agnes, you're kindness itself. You know, I never get anything like this nowadays . . . George, try one.

[*All three help themselves to a pickled onion.*]

AGNES [*with mouth full*]: Well, I must say it's good to see you again, sir, for all you've come up in the world. All the same, I shall never get used to your being Pope, never. Oh, I hope you don't think I don't know my place!

HADRIAN [*rising*]: Your place, Agnes, is always close to Our heart.

AGNES [*also rising*]: Well, I mustn't detain you, Mr Rolfe, so I'll be getting along just as soon as You give me a blessing and say a bit of a prayer. Thank you, sir, for all you've done and I'll say a prayer for you every day for as long as I'm spared. [*She gets, with some difficulty, to her knees, and receives the Pontifical Blessing.*]

HADRIAN [*causing her to rise*]: Are you going back at once, Agnes?

AGNES: Well, I was thinking of having a bit of a look-round before going back. It's silly to come all this way and not see the sights.

HADRIAN: Then take this card. [*He takes out his huge fountain-pen and writes.*] You give this card to the 'fancy gentleman' who is going to take you downstairs and tell him what you want to see.

AGNES: Will they want me to give the card up at the door?

HADRIAN: Not if you want to keep it.

AGNES: I'll keep this card till I'm laid out. God bless you, my dear. [*She kisses the* POPE'*s ring and trots out.*]

[HADRIAN *watches her go. Then he starts to walk up and down in some inner foment. Suddenly he stops and slams his clenched fist hard into a mirror.*]

HADRIAN: Filthy hypocrite! [*Then, after a pause, sucks his bleeding knuckles and smiles gently to himself.*]

[TALACRYN *enters with unusual lack of formality. He obviously bears urgent news.*]

TALA [*breathing heavily*]: Forgive my precipitance, Holiness, but the news I bring ... is of the greatest urgency.

HADRIAN [*still unconcerned*]: You're quite breathless, Frank. A man of your weight must take care. [*He taps his heart significantly.*]

TALA: Holiness, please let me be serious. Calumnies have been published. Terrible things have been said.

HADRIAN [*freezing*]: Oh? What sort of things? By whom? Who has published them?

TALA: Malignant things referring to Your Holiness's secular life. Published in an Ulster newspaper, and worse –

HADRIAN: Yes?

TALA: In a prominent journal sponsored by the Church.

HADRIAN: Who has written this? What has been said?

[RAGNA *swirls in triumphantly bearing a sheaf of newspapers.*]

RAGNA: Perhaps these will inform Your Holiness. [*He passes the papers to* HADRIAN.] Your Holiness is well qualified to appreciate the validity of your English newspapers.

HADRIAN [*with extreme frigidity*]: Light a lamp please. We cannot see in the dark.

[TALACRYN *lights a table lamp.* HADRIAN, *shielding his eyes with his left hand, takes up a paper and starts to read.*]

RAGNA: These English newspapers have been too much trouble. Suddenly they find it very interesting to make study of the life of the English Pope. They find very interesting things.

HADRIAN [*still reading. Half to himself*]: Things unanswerable because the merest whisper distorts the truth . . .

RAGNA: The English reporters are careful to begin at the beginning – His Holiness was expelled from ecclesiastical college in Roma because he is owing everybody money. He makes friends with old Italian lady, the Duchess of Sforza-Cesarini, who is very rich.

HADRIAN [*to himself*]: Unanswerable because it is half-truth.

RAGNA: Back in England, His Holiness becomes 'Baron Corvo', a fine gentleman who inherited title from his noble Italian friend. He use title to gain influence and obtain more money.

HADRIAN [*still to himself*]: Half-truth again. Who could have attacked with such malign ingenuity?

RAGNA: The Baron tries to buy some property, but people find he is not 'Baron'. He has no money to buy property. He is a fraud, an adventurer.

HADRIAN [*searching the column*]: Anonymous! Anonymous half-truths. I should be able to recognize the filthy paw of this muck-raker.

RAGNA: So 'Baron Corvo' runs away; to another town where he makes more trouble and owes more money; this time in Wales.

HADRIAN: We were not in Wales at this time, but in Belfast. Yes, of course – Sant. Jeremiah Sant!

RAGNA: But in Ireland it is also the same story; he is again the great gentleman; the writer, photographer, inventor of many things, a friend of many famous people. But it is all lies. He has no money. He has no friends. He is nothing. He owe money to the people where he is living. They take him from bed and put him into the street. They throw his clothes after him so he must dress in the street.

[TALACRYN *reacts sharply at this humiliating revelation.*]

HADRIAN [*looking up at* RAGNA]: Yes, We appear to be a very disreputable character, do We not. But We demand, Lord Cardinal, that you take note of certain errors.

RAGNA: Errors in Your English newspapers?

HADRIAN: . . . ten, eleven, twelve, thirteen, fourteen, fifteen . . . why should English newspapers be less corrupt than Italian? Fifteen absolute and deliberate lies, in a column and a half of print . . . Well, Lord Cardinal?

RAGNA [*getting angry*]: Very well, you tell me this is all lies. But today the whole world is reading these papers. What are You going to do?

HADRIAN [*icily*]: We will ponder the matter Your Eminence has set before Us, and at a convenient time We will declare Our pleasure.

RAGNA [*almost apoplectic*]: Convenient time, eh? Declare your pleasure, eh? Let me remind Your Holiness that I am Cardinal Secretary of State of the Vatican and I demand to know what you are going to do.

HADRIAN: Your Eminence shall hear. You now have Our permission to retire.

[RAGNA *pauses, then sweeps out.*]

HADRIAN [*to* TALACRYN]: Please, will Your Lordship leave Us also.

TALA: If Your Holiness should want us – at any hour . . .

[TALACRYN *goes.* HADRIAN *pauses for a moment. Then he goes down on his knees.*]

[*Sign of cross.*] All right, Lord, it is my own fault. I have not loved my neighbour in the past. I have been hard, austere, unkind – rubbed salt into wounds with biting words and satire, and sarcasm, and corrosive irony as well I know how to.

But Lord, until now I have been fighting stark-naked and alone against seemingly impossible odds. No matter. It was part of the struggle for the life which You gave me. Now I humbly thank you for giving me punishment in this world. But above all – above all, Lord, I thank you for giving me something that I have never had before – something that transcends all misfortune that can possibly touch me on this earth: You have opened to me the path of Love. [*Pause*] I would like to go to sleep now, Lord. I am very tired.

LIGHTS FADE

Scene Five

And come up on
The Throne Room in Vatican.
A number of CARDINALS *are assembled including* TALACRYN,
COURTLEIGH, RAGNA, BERSTEIN, ST ALBANS, *and as many*
others as possible. The Throne is empty.

COURT [*referring to newspapers*]: Personally, I've never read anything more abominable in my life.

RAGNA [*angry*]: Abominable! It is also abominable that the Holy See is brought in disrepute. I tell Your Eminences, in the face of such a scandal, there is only one thing. His Holiness must abdicate.

COURT: I very much doubt if he will do what Your Lordship suggests. He says that it is not the Pope who is aspersed, but Frederick William Rolfe.

ST ALBANS: That's drawing it rather fine – even for a Jesuit.

COURT: Fine enough, I think.

BERSTEIN: I do not like this reasoning. Unless the scandals are effectively repudiated it is the Pope who is held up to public ridicule, and now that we have lost the Temporal power ...

RAGNA: *Bene* ... so why does He not make a public statement to the newspapers? Why does He not excommunicate the Catholic editor? He has authority. There is the Papal Bull 'Exsecrabilis' of Pio Secund. 'Exsecrabilis'! A very nice Bull. Why he does not use this?

TALA: His Holiness is a most incomprehensible creature. He will not move in the matter and I doubt if Your Lordships will persuade Him to alter his purpose.

[HADRIAN *enters swiftly and takes his place on the Throne.*
He looks paler than usual, and older. The CARDINALS *pay*

conventional respects. All, in their different ways, show their reactions to the publication of the calumnies either by curiosity or sympathy or silent antagonism.]

HADRIAN [*taut but composed*]: Lord Cardinals. We have summoned you that ye may speak your minds. We think that there are many things which ye desire to know. We, on Our part, are ready to hear and to respond.

[*There is a pause while their Eminences look down or fidget in silence.*]

Be ye reminded that The Servant of the servants of God must not fear to soil the whiteness of His robe.

[*The* CARDINALS *keep silence still.*]

Very well then. [*He leaps up and significantly draws off the the Pontifical ring and puts it on the seat of the Throne. He walks round and rests his hands on the back of the Throne. Dropping Pontifical manner.*] Gentlemen, would some of you like to put Frederick William Rolfe to the question?

[*After an embarrassed pause, there is a general murmur of assent.*]

RAGNA: We ask for statement concerning scandals in many English and Catholic newspapers. [*He waves sheaf of clippings.*]

HADRIAN: I believe I'm aware of what Your Eminence refers to.

COURT: We – that is – many of us feel that Your Holiness has been grossly misrepresented. We would appreciate a statement to refute these calumnies.

HADRIAN [*in voice of icy reticence*]: Very well. I will give to the Sacred College that statement. And when I shall have finished speaking I never will return to this subject.

COURT: Then if Your Holiness would enlighten –

HADRIAN: There is no Holiness here.

COURT [*bowing acknowledgement*]: One confesses that the question of the pseudonyms is of interest.

HADRIAN: Pseudonyms: when I was kicked out of St Andrew's

College without a farthing or a friend, I was obliged to live by my wits. Thank God who gave me wits to live by. Think of this: I was a tonsured clerk forced to earn a living by secular means, but always intending to persist in my Divine Vocation. I had a shuddering repugnance from associating my name, the name by which some day I should be known in the priesthood, with secular pursuits, so I adopted a pseudonym. But as time went on and Catholic malfeasance drove me from one trade to another, I split up my personality and carried on each trade under a separate pseudonym: as Baron Corvo I wrote and painted and photographed; as F. Austin I designed decorations; as Frank Hochheimer I did journalism. There were four at least. Four entities careering round like colts in a meadow dissipating energy which, but for the imbecility of the Church, could have been canalized to fulfil its proper purpose years ago.

RAGNA [*tapping his sheaf of press cuttings*]: What about the debts? Perhaps you explain the debts, please.

HADRIAN: Debts! From the moment they were first contracted with the connivance and consent of certain prelates not unknown to some of you here –

[COURTLEIGH *and* TALACRYN *show signs of embarrassment.*]

– debts were never off my chest for twenty years. I was foolish enough to believe that you Catholics would keep your promises and pay me for the work which I did at your orders. So I accepted credit. I worked – God knows how I worked – and expected a just wage. When it was withheld people encouraged me to hope and work on. They offered me the odd guinea to go on with. I took the filthy guinea. God forgive me for becoming so degraded. But one can't pay one's debts and lead a Godly life for ever after on an occasional guinea. My weakness, my fault was that I did not die, murdered at St Andrew's College.

BERSTEIN: Perhaps you will now condescend to explain allegations of luxurious living –

TALA: Holy Father, don't say another word. [*Turning to his colleagues*] Shame on you! How can you torture the man so! Can't you see what you're doing, wracking the poor soul like this. Pulling him in little pieces all over again.

[*Sounds of assent from several*]

BERSTEIN: I think it would be in the best interest if we were to hear everything.

COURT: Surely, my Lords, we have heard enough –

HADRIAN: But you shall hear more. They say that I gorged myself with sumptuous banquets at grand hotels. Once after several days of starvation, I got a hard-earned, begrudging and overdue fee from a magazine. I went and had an omelette at a small-town commercial doss-house which called itself 'The Grand Hotel'. They also say that, in my lodgings, I demanded elaborate dishes to be made from my own cookery book. Since I was beholden to my landlords I did indeed ask for special dishes – dishes of lentils and carrots – I do not touch meat – anything that was cheapest, cleanest, easiest and most filling. Each dish cost a few pence and I sometimes had one each day. And occasionally when I earned a little bit I spent a few shillings on apparatus conducive to personal cleanliness, soap, baths and so on. That is the story of my luxurious living, my Lords.

[*There is a pause and all keep silent.*]

I have been provoked, abused, calumniated, traduced with insinuation, innuendo, misrepresentation, lies; my life has been held up to ridicule and to most inferior contempt. I tell you this because officially I must correct an error. You may take it or leave it as an example of how your Catholics, laymen and clergy alike, can tire out and drive almost to death a man's body – perhaps even his soul. But understand this, my Lords: by no word will I ever defend myself outside these walls. Nor do I speak in my own defence, Venerable

Fathers, even to you. I, personally and of predilection am indifferent to opinions, but it is your right to hear that which you have heard.

[*There is silence again. Then* RAGNA *speaks out.*]

RAGNA [*waving press cuttings*]: 'An enemy hath done this.'

HADRIAN [*with candid delight*]: Those are the first genuine words which I have heard from Your Eminence's heart.

RAGNA [*voice of thunder*]: Who is it has done this evil thing?

TALA: A reactionary blackmailer and a disappointed woman – two worms that have turned.

RAGNA [*roaring*]: *Anathema sint*: Let them be smothered in the dung-hill.

[*Slowly* HADRIAN *returns to be seated on his Throne. He takes up the Pontifical ring and puts it on his finger.*]

HADRIAN [*in Pontifical manner*]: Lord Cardinals, it is Our wish to be alone.

[*The* CARDINALS *withdraw severally.* RAGNA *is the last to leave.* HADRIAN *calls him back.*]

Lord Cardinal.

RAGNA [*turning*]: Holiness?

HADRIAN: May We detain you a moment longer?

RAGNA [*returning*]: Please, Holiness.

HADRIAN [*with warmth and charm, in contrast to his earlier manner*]: We are happy to think that Your Eminence is no longer opposed to Us.

RAGNA [*responding warmly*]: I too am happy, Most Holy Father, that God has opened my eyes to the injustices done to Your Holiness. I beg that Your Holiness will forgive me for blindness in the past.

HADRIAN [*deceptively docile*]: Your Eminence is already forgiven. We are particularly pleased to have your Lordship's co-operation at the present time since there is a matter particularly close to Our heart on which We would welcome your advice.

RAGNA: Pray open your heart, Most Holy Father.

HADRIAN: Very well. [*No bomb was ever dropped more gently.*]
By way of emphasizing the essential difference between the
Church Temporal – which We have already renounced – and
the Church Apostolic, We have in mind to give away the
Vatican Treasure.

RAGNA [*shaken*]: The Vatican Treasure! But has Your Holiness
considered that most of the treasures are consecrated to the
service of the Church.

HADRIAN: Oh, that! There seems little point in keeping costly
baubles locked up in cupboards. Sotheby's can take care of
all that.

RAGNA: I find myself a little slow to comprehend your Holiness's –

HADRIAN: I'm talking about our Real Estate in Manhattan.

RAGNA: Manhattan! But has Your Holiness had time to consider that even the smallest piece of this property – so – (He
demonstrates roughly a square metre) is worth many thousands of dollars?

HADRIAN: Yes, and has your Lordship, with your many
important preoccupations, had time to consider that the
Church exists for God in His creatures. She does not serve
either by charging extortionate rents to a lot of Wall Street
brokers.

RAGNA: Ay, ay, ay!

HADRIAN: Well, my Lord? Are you with Us or against Us?

RAGNA [*after a pause*]: Holy Father, I am with You with all my
heart. Under Your inspired guidance let the Church once
more meet the World in the pure missionary spirit of Her
greatest days. I shall follow wherever Your Holiness may
lead.

HADRIAN: God bless Your Eminence for that. To tell the
truth, I was in no mood for another fight.

[*They both laugh.*]

Your Eminence, may I now suggest that you accompany Us
to St John Lateran?

RAGNA: *Va bene.* With great pleasure, Most Holy Father.

HADRIAN: They will be saying prayers there for those having authority in the Church. It would seem to be a suitable occasion to celebrate our reconciliation.

RAGNA: *Benissimo.* Will Your Holiness go by carriage or in the *sedia gestatoria*?

HADRIAN: Perhaps Your Eminence is in the mood to indulge Our English eccentricities even further?

RAGNA [*walking into the trap*]: With pleasure, Holiness. Of course.

HADRIAN [*with a smile*]: Then we will walk.

RAGNA [*aghast*]: Walk! But Holiness –

HADRIAN: Your Eminence did say you would follow where-ever We may lead.

[HADRIAN *claps his hands and* ROSE *appears.*]

HADRIAN: My sunshade, George. Cardinal Ragna is walking with Us to Lateran.

RAGNA: But, Holy Father, the political situation is very, very dangerous.

[ROSE *hands sunshade to* HADRIAN.]

HADRIAN [*still smiling*]: Quite. But as We mentioned to Your Eminence once before –

RAGNA [*raising his hands to Heaven*]: But, Holiness, I am too fat to become a martyr.

[HADRIAN *opens the white Pontifical sunshade with its green lining.*]

HADRIAN: My Lord Cardinal, in every fat priest, there is always a bony martyr crying out for Beatitude.

HADRIAN *leads off, followed by the now faithful* RAGNA, *crossing himself and tut-tutting.*

LIGHTS CHANGE

Scene Six

HADRIAN's *room in Vatican. Enter* SWISS GUARDS *who take up* 'on guard' *positions round the room. They are followed by* CHAMBERLAINS *escorting* SANT *and* MRS CROWE. *The former attempts a truculent nonchalance, the latter is obviously nervous. The* SENIOR CHAMBERLAIN *seats them in two chairs placed facing an empty Throne and then withdraws. There is a silence in which* SANT *and* CROWE *sit awkwardly facing a ring of implacable* SWITZERS.

MRS CROWE [*in stage whisper*]: Oh, dear. Why don't they hurry up. Oh, I do wish I'd never come.

SANT [*also in stage whisper*]: Shut up, Nancy. Do you want them to hear you?

MRS CROWE: I just wish it was all over, that's all.

SANT: Can't you see that's just what he wants. He wants to get us rattled. But I'll rattle him first. [*Chinks his loose change in pocket.*] Ay.

MRS CROWE: Oh, I do hope you're right, Jerry.

SANT: Of course I am. You don't imagine I gave the papers all I know, do you? Not by a long chalk I didn't. Not by a very long chalk. He'll listen to me this time, or my name's not Jeremiah Sant.

[*The* SWITZERS *come to attention and* HADRIAN *enters, followed by* RAGNA, COURTLEIGH, TALACRYN, *and* FATHER ROSE. SANT *forgets himself and automatically makes to rise, then, remembering, sits down again insolently.* HADRIAN *assumes the Throne flanked by the* CARDINALS. FATHER ROSE *sits at small table near* HADRIAN *and prepares to write in shorthand notebook.* HADRIAN *makes a gesture dismissing* GUARDS *who file off stage.*]

HADRIAN [*frigid, but without menace*]: We have summoned you in order that ye may speak your mind to Us. But Our

74

Utterances and yours shall be recorded. [*He indicates* FR
ROSE.]

SANT: I object. This was to be a private interview.

HADRIAN: In order to start in a conciliatory atmosphere, We
concede. [*To* MRS CROWE] Madam, what do you want?

[MRS CROWE *manifests acute agitation and embarrassment.*]

MRS CROWE: Well, you know why I came here. I – er . . . I –
er . . . [*She looks desperately to* SANT *for a lead.*]

SANT: I think it would be more advantageous to all parties if
I was to speak for Mrs Crowe.

HADRIAN: We will concede this point also. Sir, we have received your questionable letter – are aware of your calumnies
in the newspapers – and are now at a loss to know what more
you could want of Us.

SANT: Want? Well, I want reparation – damages as you might
say.

HADRIAN: For what?

SANT: Why, for the loss of time while I've had to be here, and
for my business which I've been obliged to neglect while I've
been kept waiting.

HADRIAN: To what extent have you suffered?

SANT: To what extent? Well, that shouldn't be difficult. I've
been here since last July. Say eight months, and I generally
allow a pound a day expenses. But it's cost me a sight more.
You can add five hundred pounds for out-of-pockets. Then
there's the business: say a year with salary and commission –
call it three thousand. Then there's what we'll call damages –
[*Significantly*] if you know what I mean. Well, including
'damages' you might tot it all up together and call it – twenty
thousand pounds.

HADRIAN: And your companion?

SANT: Well, better say double it. Forty thousand pounds spot
cash in sterling and we'll cry quits.

[HADRIAN *takes a look round upon his* CARDINALS *who
return it.*]

75

HADRIAN: You are demanding that We should pay you forty thousand pounds?

SANT: That's correct.

HADRIAN: Why do you demand this sum of Us?

SANT: Why? I would have thought I'd made my meaning plain. Do you want bells on it?

MRS CROWE [*obsequious*]: Perhaps if I could have a private word with His Holiness . . .

HADRIAN: Daughter, your notorious conduct debars you from a private conversation with any clergyman except in the open confessional.

MRS CROWE: Oh, I see! So it's like that, is it? Well, I think you're going to regret what you've just said. Mr Sant was quite right about you. You must be shown up for what you really are. [*To* SANT] Jerry, you tell him.

SANT [*gruffly, to* MRS CROWE]: Now just take it easy, will you. [*To* HADRIAN] I'm afraid the lady is a wee bit upset, as well she might be. And I expect she is a bit embarrassed by the presence of so many people. Could we not dispense with those fine-looking gentlemen? [*Points to the* CARDINALS.]

HADRIAN [*to* CARDINALS]: Your Eminences will be so good as to retire.

COURT: Holiness, remember You are Sovereign within these walls.

RAGNA: I will tell the Chamberlains to take these people away.

HADRIAN: No. We thank Your Lordships, but We are conducting this interview. Have no fear, since We have none.

[*The* CARDINALS *leave*, RAGNA *making gestures of despair*.]

HADRIAN: And now . . .

SANT: Now, sir, I should like to make an end to this matter and I dare say you've other things to be getting on with yourself. Suppose you make a suggestion. I don't think you'll find us unreasonable.

HADRIAN [*with deceptive mildness*]: You ask that We should pay you forty thousand pounds – spot cash was the term you used – for damages which you say We have caused.

SANT: Aye, that's right.

HADRIAN: It's useless to point out to you that We did not ask you to waste your time in Rome.

SANT: In Rome! Not likely.

HADRIAN: And that We did not force you or induce you to neglect your business?

SANT [*getting angry*]: No. But I dare say you were banking on it that I'd never dare face you, weren't ye? If ye'd have had the civility to have answered my letters and made an appointment like I suggested a while back, we'd have had this settled and done with without all this unpleasantness.

HADRIAN: For the credit of the human race, it must be said that indecent exhibitions of this kind are rare. But some men are gifted with an abnormal capacity for making fools of themselves. Mr Sant, does it not occur to you that you are engaging in foolish and singularly dirty business?

SANT [*practically out of his chair*]: Who d'ye think you're talking to? My hands are as clean as yours any day. Who skipped owing this lady here her rent, ay? Well, go on ...

[HADRIAN *turns to* FR ROSE *who produces a receipt from a file on his lap.* HADRIAN *takes it and proffers it to* MRS CROWE *who disdains it with a shrug.* SANT *snatches it.*

HADRIAN: You know, Madam, that We paid this bill the moment We were in a position to do so.

SANT: Well, if you've paid her why shouldn't you pay me?

HADRIAN: Because We owe you nothing.

SANT: So that's the way of it is it? Then you'll be wanting to see a bit more about yer scabby little self in the papers then?

FR ROSE [*rising to his feet*]: Let me call the guard, Holiness.

HADRIAN: No.

[FR ROSE *resumes his seat apprehensively.*]

[*to* SANT]: Listen, Mr Sant, We look upon you as a deeply injured man –

SANT: That's more like it.

77

HADRIAN: – injured only by himself.

SANT: What?

HADRIAN: You have suffered loss and damage only because of your persistence in doing evil things. In this you have been your own enemy.

SANT: Me own *what*? You sit there and tell me –

HADRIAN [*raising his voice*]: Mr Sant. Is it useless to ask you to change. You shall be helped. You will not be left alone.

SANT [*shouting*]: I want what I come here to get – my money.

HADRIAN: If you wish honestly to earn a better living, we shall give you that opportunity.

SANT [*rising*]: The hell with that. What about damages for the past?

HADRIAN [*also rising*]: We promise you a chance for the future.

SANT [*with menace*]: You won't pay, then?

HADRIAN: On your terms – not one farthing. But We will help you to save your soul.

SANT [*he is almost out of his mind*]: You'll save *my* soul? You!

MRS CROWE [*urgently*]: Jerry, sit down – please.

SANT [*looks back at* HADRIAN]: You make me – sick, you dirty Taigh.

MRS CROWE [*desperately she gets up*]: Jerry, I want to go. Please. It's no good.

SANT [*he takes a pace towards* HADRIAN]: He's just a little insect. [*To* HADRIAN.] Aren't ye?

MRS CROWE: Jerry, please . . .
      [FR ROSE *gets up in alarm.*]

FR ROSE [*shouting*]: Guard! *Presto! Presto!*

SANT [*quite out of his mind now, draws a revolver*]: And ye know what to do with insects, don't ye? Tread them underfoot.

MRS CROWE [*shrieks*]: Jerry!

SANT: Vengeance is mine, Saith the Lord! Halleluya!
      [SWISS GUARDS, *not knowing what is required of them, rush in shouting* 'Pronto! Pronto!' (*ad lib*).]

78

[*Before anyone knows what is happening,* SANT *fires once.* HADRIAN *stands quite still.* FR ROSE, *knocking over his desk, rushes forward. The* GUARDS' *reactions are slower, but they follow.* SANT *fires for the second time and* MRS CROWE *screams.* HADRIAN *remains still, though he seems to sway. As* SANT *fires for the third time,* FR ROSE *tries to interpose himself between* SANT *and* HADRIAN. *He fails but manages to catch his master who now slowly subsides as a patch of crimson defiles the apostolic whiteness of his robe.*

RAGNA, TALACRYN *and others rush in.*

The GUARDS *overpower* SANT *half-killing him and hold him on the floor. All eyes turn to* HADRIAN, *who is supported by* TALACRYN *on one side and* RAGNA *on the other. The* GUARDS *fling* SANT *onto his knees before the dying Pope.*]

HADRIAN [*weakly*]: Father forgive them for they know not ... [*He struggles for breath.*] ... what they ... Venerable Fathers, Our will and pleasure is ...

TALA: Speak it, Most Holy Father.

HADRIAN: Venerable Fathers, We name you all the ministers of Our will. [*He turns towards the prisoner,* SANT.] Son, you are forgiven. You are free.

[SANT *is dragged away by the* GUARDS, *and the hysterical* MRS CROWE *with him.*]

HADRIAN: George, are you hurt? [*Unclasping his pectoral cross and giving it to* FR ROSE] Dear son, take this cross.

[FR ROSE *does so and backs away weeping.* TALACRYN *and* RAGNA *now beckon others to support the Pontiff's body, and prepare to administer final absolution. The stage fills with* MEMBERS OF THE SACRED COLLEGE *and others.*]

TALA [*in a whisper, overcome with emotion*]: The profession of faith, Most Holy Lord.

HADRIAN: I believe all that which Holy Mother Church believes. I ask pardon of all men ... Dear Jesus, be not to me a judge but a Saviour.

TALA: Saints of God, advance to help him. Angels of the Lord

79

come to meet him, receiving his soul, offering it in the Sight of the Most High.

[HADRIAN, *earthly Vicar of Christ, receives Extreme Unction. He then indicates his wish to be lifted on his feet. He is raised by* CARDINAL TALACRYN *and* CARDINAL VAN KRISTEN. *The blood streams down the dying Pontiff's white robes. He slowly raises his right hand which can hardly bear the weight of two huge Pontifical rings.*]

HADRIAN: May My God Omnipotent, [*The Sign of the Cross.*] Father, [*The Sign of the Cross.*] Son, [*The Sign of the Cross.*] and Holy Ghost, bless you.

[*He dies. A bell begins a solemn toll.*]

TALA: God have mercy on his soul.

[*Four* SWITZERS *take up his body and lay it on a bier.* PRIESTS *and* PRELATES *group round it and pray.*

The stage darkens till the bier is lit only by four candles. FR ROSE *crosses down stage so that he is clearly seen.*]

FR ROSE: *Prosit quaesumus, Domine, animae famuli tui* Frederick William Rolfe, *Hadriane, Summi Pontificis, miseracordiae tuae implorata clementia: ut ejus, in quo speravit et credidit, aeternum capiat, te miserante, consortium. Per Dominum.*

[*He makes the Sign of the Cross.*]

Have any of you ever dissected a crab? Under its hard shell your crustacean is a labyrinthine mass of most sensitive nerves for the defence of which it is armed with crookedly-curving, ferociously-snapping claws. . . . Similarly, Frederick William Rolfe, Baron Carvo, as hard as adamant outside, was, within, the tenderest, the most sensitive, the cleverest, the unhappiest, the most dreadful of all creatures. Yet he tolerated the most fearful revilings and humiliations and, because he knew quite precisely how strong he was, he was absolutely careless as to what the world might say. But his utter fearlessness, his utterly straightforward simplicity, his utterly boundless and irresistable audacity never were understood by boobies and imbeciles. Faced with the idiocy of the vulgar and profane, the imbecility of the bovine and supine, his imperscrutable serenity and his abominable self-possession would be cast aside and the hitherto stilly-folded claws would come clashing and tearing with a violence that was sudden and frightful.

But the One cannot stand forever alone against the Many. With his unconquerable capacity for endurance he struggled on, making himself a most accented nuisance to those who rose up and filled the circumambient air with howls at his infinite potency until, in the end, nothing was left in him, except the desire to feel the touch of sweet white death.

And so it happened. So died Hadrian the Seventh, Bishop, Servant of the Servants of God – and maybe Martyr.

[*As lights fade,* ROLFE, *as we saw him at the beginning of act one, walks on and watches with approval the funeral cortège carrying out* HADRIAN's *bier. He is smoking a cigarette and he carries in his arms a huge bundle of manuscript.*]

FR ROSE ⎫
ROLFE ⎭ (*together*): Let us pray for the repose of his soul. He was so tired.

LIGHTING CHANGE

Scene Seven

ROLFE's *room in London as at beginning of act one.* ROLFE *is seated at his table, with his manuscript beside him. There is a knock at the door.*

MRS CROWE: Mr Rolfe.

ROLFE: What is it?

[MRS CROWE *enters.*]

MRS CROWE: I came up to tell you that there's the two men downstairs called to see you again.

[ROLFE *looks blank for a moment.*]

ROLFE: What?

MRS CROWE [*with meaning*]: You know.

[ROLFE *pauses in thought for a second. Then:*]

ROLFE [*eagerly*]: Oh yes, of course. Their Lordships. Show them up, please.

MRS CROWE [*dubiously*]: Very well, then.

[*As soon as she has gone,* ROLFE *tries to make himself more respectable. He stands erect to receive his visitors. In a minute they enter. It is the two* BAILIFFS. *The younger holds a Warrant of Execution in his hand. The old one smiles amiably.*]

1ST BAILIFF: Mr Corvo?

ROLFE [*scarcely audible*]: No.

1ST BAILIFF: Sorry, sir, *Baron* Corvo.

ROLFE [*icily*]: That is not my name.

1ST BAILIFF [*consulting papers*]: Of course, sir. You are Mr Frederick William Rolfe.

[ROLFE *stands erect but one knee begins to tremble. The* BAILIFFS *push past him into the room and walk round it in circles, appraising its pitiful contents with professional eyes.*]

1ST BAILIFF: You were warned, Mr Rolfe. I did warn you, didn't I?

[ROLFE *stands rigid saying nothing.*]

Now I am afraid we shall be obliged to distrain your effects in accordance with this Warrant of Execution.

[*Still* ROLFE *says nothing.*]

You, do comprehend, don't you Mr Rolfe, that we are acting with the authority of a Warrant issued by the Court?

[ROLFE *still remains silent and immobile.*]

2ND BAILIFF [*who has been wandering round the room*]: A Warrant of Execution . . . [*He comes to the table.*] I'm afraid this'll have to go too, Sir.

1ST BAILIFF: Mmm – yes . . . [*He comes to the table with the pile of manuscripts on it. He looks at it suspiciously.*] *Hadrian the Seventh?* What's this then?

ROLFE: A book.

2ND BAILIFF: Write books, do you?

[ROLFE *does not deign to answer.*]

1ST BAILIFF: What's it about then?

ROLFE: About? . . . It's about a man who made the fatuous and frantic mistake of living before his time.

1ST BAILIFF: Any value?

ROLFE: It's a masterpiece and, therefore, probably not worth tuppence.

[*The* TWO BAILIFFS *exchange glances of incomprehension.*]

ROLFE: At the same time, it is possibly beyond price.

[ROLFE *lays his hands gently on the MS. The* BAILIFFS *look more than ever confused.*]

1ST BAILIFF [*to his colleague*]: All right then, let's get these out. [*Together the* BAILIFFS *take out the table and chair.* ROLFE *stands quite still, holding his MS. After a moment the* 1ST BAILIFF *comes in again, crosses to* ROLFE, *takes the MS and makes towards the door.*]

1ST BAILIFF: Best not to take any chances, Mr Rolfe. After all, you could be right. [*He goes.*]

ROLFE *is left all alone in the bare room, standing rigidly as he has done from the moment the moment the bailiffs came in. As he stands there, one knee begins to tremble violently.*

CURTAIN